If These WALLS *Could* TALK:
NEW YORK METS

If These **WALLS** *Could* **TALK:**
NEW YORK METS

Stories from the
New York Mets Dugout,
Locker Room, and Press Box

Mike Puma

TRIUMPH
B O O K S

Library of Congress Cataloging-in-Publication Data

Names: Puma, Mike, 1970- author.
Title: If these walls could talk : New York Mets : stories from the New York Mets dugout, locker room, and press box / Mike Puma.
Description: Chicago, Illinois : Triumph Books, [2021] | Series: If these walls could talk
Identifiers: LCCN 2021058772 | ISBN 9781629377742 (paperback) | ISBN 9781641256100 (epub)
Subjects: LCSH: New York Mets (Baseball team)—Anecdotes. | New York Mets (Baseball team)—History. | Baseball teams—New York (State)—New York. | Baseball—United States—History.
Classification: LCC GV875.N45 P86 2021 | DDC 796.357/64097471—dc23
LC record available at https://lccn.loc.gov/2021058772

This book is available in quantity at special discounts for your group or organization. For further information, contact:

Triumph Books LLC
814 North Franklin Street
Chicago, Illinois 60610
(312) 337-0747
www.triumphbooks.com

Printed in U.S.A.
ISBN: 978-1-62937-774-2
Design by Amy Carter
Page production by Nord Compo
Photos courtesy of Getty Images unless otherwise indicated

CONTENTS

FOREWORD

As my character Jim Brockmire likes to say, "The Mets are the Yankees of not being the Yankees." While that is a joke, it does seem kind of true. As great, classy, and wonderful as the Yankees are (or at least seem), the Mets have been equally as hapless, unfortunate, and circuslike. Maybe that will begin changing under Steve Cohen's ownership.

Growing up in the 1970s, it was the Yankees that really had the circus atmosphere with those Reggie Jackson/Billy Martin teams, but with a tradition of winning that went along with it. Sure, the Yanks had some rough stretches, in the late 1960s and the '80s, but those are the exception. The exception for the Mets is when they do well, like in 2015 or in the Subway Series of 2000 or certainly in 1986. But the baseline for Mets fans is, "How is it going to go wrong?"

Full disclosure: I loved both teams as a kid. I didn't start hating the Yankees and choosing a side until the 2000 Subway Series, particularly the moment when Roger Clemens threw the bat at Mike Piazza.

Rich Eisen, now of NFL Network, is a good friend of mine, and before I became friends with him, he reported on ESPN that Jason Giambi had been signed by the Yankees. When I heard that, I yelled at the TV: "Hey! How come *we* can't get Giambi?!" And Rich Eisen right after that literally said on the air, "I can just hear all the Mets fans now going, 'Hey! How come *we* can't get Giambi?!'" A great Mets tradition that I hope has passed: bitterness over the seemingly endless and pocket-bottomless Yankees free-agent signings.

I didn't even realize I *had* to pick a team as a New Yorker until much later in life. Ironically, I moved to Los Angeles in 1986 (the last time the Mets won the World Series)—and stayed there for 27 years. Back then it wasn't so easy to follow your team remotely. There was no satellite or MLB package or a team web page. You were a slave to local coverage and had to look up box scores in the newspaper to see what was going on. I lived in L.A. long enough that I considered becoming a Dodgers fan. I love baseball and I got a Dodgers game every night, the great Vin Scully in the booth, and Dodger Talk always on the radio.

One spring training, probably around 1990, I decided to follow all the Dodgers storylines and completely educate myself on them the same way I always knew the Mets. All through spring training, I learned who the new guys were, the injuries, everything. There it was, Opening Day, I was all excited for the new season. *Here we go with a full season of baseball I care about!* The first pitch was thrown, and…*Wow, I don't care.* I bleed orange and blue, not Dodgers blue.

Similarly, over the years I have often seen the logic in liking the Yankees more than the Mets. It would be much easier emotionally. I've tried to do it, justifying it by saying that when I was a kid I really *did* love the Yankees, too, but again and alas, I bleed orange and blue. Not Yankees black, or navy, or whatever the heck color that is.

* * *

The Mets' collapse of 2007 is the only time I can remember being depressed for a prolonged period based on a sports result. I almost got a little concerned for myself. The fall of '07 was like a nightmare from which I couldn't awaken, and then to have it happen again—not quite as dramatically, but almost—the following year was just beyond awful, even for a Mets fan. And that was coming off the tremendous disappointment of 2006, with the great Endy Chavez catch leading to Carlos Beltran leaving his bat on his shoulder for strike three.

I'm one of those Mets fans who never forgave Beltran, by the way. When he got hired as Mets manager I was against it for no other reason than I still have post-traumatic stress disorder over the image of that bat on his shoulder. Yeah, yeah, I know; he was a great Mets player and it's probably childish to hold a grudge like that. But that is one of the few perks of being a Mets fan: holding on dearly to childish grudges. I also hold one toward Tom Glavine for that final loss in 2007 and then seemingly not caring about it in the press conference afterward. Only Mets fans are torn over whom they dislike more—hated rivals like Chipper Jones and Chase Utley, or their own guys who let them down (*cough* Bay/Familia/Diaz/Harvey *cough*).

Life as a Mets fan has completely colored my worldview. I'm in show business and it's very speculative. Every venture is a gamble. It's very hard to get anything made—even my recent show *Brockmire* took about 10 years to bring to life. There's many turns in the road in any project where things are in doubt. At the first sign of trouble, I'm always like, *Well, that's it, we're never going to pull this off.* My partners often ask me why I'm so negative, pessimistic, and sure that the worst-case scenario is inevitable. "BECAUSE I'M A METS FAN!" I yell. Then when they laugh, I yell, "I'M NOT KIDDING!"

My son is 11 years old and I'm only half-joking when I say that I moved back to New York because I wanted to raise a Mets fan. I feel I need support in my old age in this avocation. I can't face it alone. I have more than a little guilt that I made him a Mets fan. About three times a year he comes to me and says, "Dad, are you sure we can't be Yankees fans?" I tell him I'm quite sure, but I feel his pain.

But I also tell him that it *does* make the wins sweeter—the fact they are way fewer and further between for us Mets fans. The 2015 season was euphoric and delightful. It ended sadly, but along the way it featured years of built-up misery getting released. I don't know that fans of the Yankees, New England Patriots, or even the Golden State Warriors have the same kind of joy that Mets fans get when the team does well—even after just a good month, never mind a season.

I feel the Mets have to earn my watching a full game in real time. I will start out the season by watching only the first two innings in full—I want to get a feel for the team and hear what Gary Cohen, Keith Hernandez, and Ron Darling are saying. I don't like watching an opponent score on the Mets—it upsets me—so I will watch the game about an hour delayed off a recording and fast-forward when the other team is batting, unless I am really curious about how Noah Syndergaard or Jacob deGrom or whoever is throwing. I don't even watch the Mets' at-bats in real time. I just wait until there's a runner in scoring position. My method condenses watching the game to about 90 minutes. But even that version of viewing is born out of being a Mets fan—out of just being so depressed for so long over horrible losses and collapses. Lord knows we have seen enough of them.

* * *

There's been much talk about how New York comedians are often Mets and not Yankees fans. There's kind of an underdog, self-deprecating mentality to loving the Mets that I suppose lends itself to comedy. I honestly don't know which came first—meaning was I sort of a semi-depressive type and thus the Mets appealed to me? Or did becoming a Mets fan contribute to my being sort of a sad sack? It's probably a little of both.

But if comedy is born from pain and being misunderstood and feeling outside and like an underdog, well, let's just say that being a Mets fan did not do anything to alleviate any of that.

When people ask me if I'm a baseball fan, I say, "No. I'm a Mets fan. There's a difference."

—Hank Azaria

Hank Azaria is a comedian and actor best known for voicing many characters in The Simpsons *and for his role as the title character in the television show* Brockmire. *Born in New York City, he is a longtime Mets fan.*

FOREWORD

I'm ready for the Mets to win their next World Series.

As somebody who played for the franchise's last world championship team in 1986, it's nice to be recognized for helping deliver one of the only two World Series titles in team history. But we've had our day, and it can never be taken from us. I am ready to pass the baton. We are ready for a successor to the throne.

Several talented Mets teams in the 2000s had a shot at getting there but for whatever reason fell short.

Most recently, the 2015 team that reached the World Series, losing in five games to the Royals, provided us with hope the drought would end. Yoenis Cespedes helped carry the Mets to the pennant, but it's funny how that all transpired. Remember, general manager Sandy Alderson's last choice at the trade deadline was Cespedes, after other options disappeared. Cespedes kind of won by default, so maybe Sandy knew something that we didn't. There never would have been a 2015 without Cespedes, thank you very much, and the relationship is over now.

Matt Harvey was another star from that team who never again enjoyed such success. Injuries were a big part of it, but off the field he didn't help himself. Harvey put the cart before the horse. I think when Matt looks back on his life he will probably regret a lot of things. It was going to be "Matt Harvey takes Manhattan," and to be Joe Namath or Tom Seaver, you have got to have numbers. Once you fall from stardom, you know the old saying: you meet the same people on the way up as you do on the way down. There are people out there—it's human nature—who love to see failure, and Matt didn't help himself. People were waiting for him and really salivating when he was on his way down. He brought that on himself. Lesson learned, but his career is just about over now. It's a shame. He had his moments.

I always sensed that Jacob deGrom was something special, even early in his career. He pitched better when he was in trouble and still does to this day. That goes a long way. To me, it goes a lot further than having quality stuff. But if you have quality stuff and you couple that with guts, then you have got Tom Seaver, a great pitcher, and that is what deGrom has. He has become better and better and he's smart. Intelligence also separates the good from the great, and he's got that.

I also can't help but think of Terry Collins and what he brought to the organization as Mets manager. Terry was competitive and fiery, baseball lifer and baseball man to the core. I liked that about him. To prepare for our SNY broadcasts, we talked with him daily, and it was clear he learned his lessons as manager in Houston and Anaheim. He was really at that breaking point in the game when the new generation arrived. He kind of evolved and adapted, but it didn't mean he had to like it. I would have loved to play for him.

When I began my second career, in the Mets broadcast booth, Bobby Valentine was managing the team. Bobby was our third-base coach in 1984, and I loved him then; he was an extraordinary baseball man and mind who became a terrific manager. He was right there with Whitey Herzog. Bobby was a great field general and didn't make mistakes in games. He was as good a field general as you could have as far as managing a game.

Bobby left for Texas after '84, and I actually begged him to stay because I thought he was terrific. He was a great third base coach; energetic, positive, infectious in a good way. I knew he wanted to manage, but I didn't know what kind of manager he would become until he came here and I got to watch him. I certainly was not surprised because it was quite apparent he was a baseball guru.

The Mets team he took to the World Series in 2000 that lost to the Yankees wasn't the most talented, but there was great chemistry. It's a contrast to some of the teams the Mets had later on that probably should have won more with all the talent they had, but lacked cohesion.

We are in a whole different day now with the analytics revolution. My former teammates and I are in the early winter of our lives and certainly the sun has set on our generation. The game has changed radically. Analytics is the greatest change in today's game since the end of the dead ball era. Babe Ruth had that kind of impact, it changed the game. This game was pretty much the same for a long time and now it has changed.

I've known Mike Puma since he first started covering the Mets for the *New York Post*. Nobody knows this Mets era better than Mike. I have always loved his New York sense of humor and writing style. My bet is you will enjoy his first book.

—*Keith Hernandez*

Keith Hernandez is a former MLB first baseman who played with the New York Mets from 1983 to 1989. He won two World Series, one with the Mets in 1986. A five-time All-Star, Hernandez shared the 1979 NL MVP award with Willie Stargell.

INTRODUCTION

When I arrived at the *Connecticut Post* as a general assignment sports reporter in 1997, there wasn't any talk of me covering Major League Baseball. There were enough college basketball and golf assignments in the region to keep me busy, and the Jets had created a buzz with Bill Parcells' arrival as head coach, sending me in that direction on a semi-regular basis during the NFL season.

Unexpectedly, a few days before the start of the '98 baseball season, I was told the Mets would become part of my responsibilities. Bobby Valentine, born and bred in Stamford, Connecticut—about a half-hour from the newspaper's office in Bridgeport—was about to begin his second full season as the team's manager and the Mets had been surprisingly competitive the previous year. Suddenly, the Mets were becoming a story. Before long, the Yankees were added to my duties, leaving me to split the summer between Queens and the Bronx.

In retrospect, it was a magical time and place to begin a baseball writing career. The Yankees, with a historic 125-win team, won their second World Series of four in a five-year span. But the Mets were almost as intriguing, with the trade that brought Mike Piazza to town and Valentine's colorful personality that generated controversy on a regular basis.

With Valentine and general manager Steve Phillips barely on speaking terms later on, the Mets became something of a circus. It got to the point Valentine would quiz new reporters assigned to cover the team, asking them if they sided with him or Phillips. Valentine's charm and intelligence won over many, but he also had detractors within the media who openly rooted for him to fail. Phillips wasn't nearly the polarizing force, but his own internal demons may have undermined him.

By the time I got assigned to cover the Mets full time, in 2010 for the *New York Post*, the vibe was different. Instead of distrust between GM and manager, most of the tension within the organization stemmed from the owner's suite. Fred Wilpon had bought out partner Nelson

Doubleday years earlier, leaving Wilpon's son, Jeff, in position to preside over the club's day-to-day operations. The perception became Jeff Wilpon was overmatched by the job, and only adding to the fans' angst was the Wilpons' reluctance most of the time to compete on the Yankees' level financially in pursuing free agents.

A nearly decimating blow for the Wilpons occurred after the 2008 season, when much of the family's wealth disappeared with the unraveling of Bernie Madoff's Ponzi scheme. Fred Wilpon and his brother-in-law, Saul Katz, who were heavily invested with Madoff, managed to keep the team, but the purse strings tightened, leaving the Mets in a rebuild that ultimately got the franchise to the World Series in 2015, but sustaining success proved difficult.

On the pages that follow, I will take you through my two decades–plus reporting on the Mets, beginning with that '98 season that morphed into a near-miss of the World Series the following year. Then came a Subway Series, the heartbreak that gripped New York on 9/11 and the days that followed, and a mighty swing from Piazza that gave the city a reason to smile. Valentine's firing—which he says might have occurred because of an incident involving Jeff Wilpon—followed, before the Mets (after two dreadful years under Art Howe's managerial watch) resurged with an influx of talent that included Jose Reyes, David Wright, Carlos Beltran, Carlos Delgado, and Billy Wagner. For a three-year stretch beginning in 2006, the Mets had arguably as much talent as any team in baseball, but that translated into only one playoff appearance (they lost to the Cardinals in an epic Game 7 of the NLCS in 2006) before maddening collapses in successive seasons.

In the midst of the rebuild came Johan Santana's no-hitter (a first in franchise history) and the arrival of integral pieces Matt Harvey, Jacob deGrom, and Noah Syndergaard, who helped resurrect the Mets, if only for a blip. On these pages Syndergaard will make a surprising admission about the torn lat muscle he sustained in 2017 that crippled the Mets' chances of reaching the postseason for a third straight year. I conclude with Wright's ascension to team captain and his final hurrah after debilitating injuries sidetracked his career.

The fun in this project was reconnecting with so many players, managers, and executives with whom I had developed relationships over the years, whether it was bigger names such as Piazza, Wright, Wagner, and R.A. Dickey or the more obscure Mike Baxter, whose lunging catch and collision with Citi Field's left-field fence helped preserve Santana's no-hitter but may have shortened his career.

My introduction to the sports pages came as a 10-year-old growing up in Waterbury, Connecticut, who eagerly awaited his dad's arrival home from work each day with a copy of the *New York Post*. It was there I could get the real scoop on what was happening with the Yankees and football Giants, the two teams that mattered most in the Puma household.

That I eventually got to write for the *Post*, beginning in 2007 when I was hired as a general assignment sports reporter, was something of a dream fulfilled, but the goal at an earlier age was to sit in the broadcast booth and become the next Vin Scully or Marty Glickman.

I transitioned into print shortly after my graduation from Fordham University, and through the years I never gave serious consideration to writing a book. But after 20-plus seasons covering baseball and a decade exclusively on the Mets beat, I couldn't resist when presented this opportunity for a new adventure.

Hopefully the pages that follow will inform, entertain, and evoke a few emotions. Inside every Mets fan there is plenty of scar tissue, but also a rapid heartbeat that awaits the next moment of glory.

CHAPTER 1
A WILD SUBWAY RIDE

It's more than two decades later in trying to recall the details, so Bobby Valentine isn't sure if the middle finger he extended toward the press level at Shea Stadium was pushed up against his neck or the side of his cap. It might have been his shoulder.

Valentine had been skewered, mostly on WFAN, the city's all-sports radio station, throughout the day for his curious decision the previous night to bring in a right-handed reliever to face a left-handed batter in a crucial spot. It was 1998, the second year of the regular season Subway Series between the Mets and Yankees, and New York City baseball was thriving.

The reliever was Mel Rojas (whose cousin Luis would one day assume Valentine's seat as Mets manager) and Paul O'Neill the batter. O'Neill pounced on Rojas' first pitch, a hanging forkball, and launched a three-run homer to left-center in the seventh inning that buried the Mets.

After the Mets' loss, Valentine explained the right-hander Rojas was actually a better pitcher against lefties than righties. Rojas' statistics for that season and his career backed that claim. But in this pre-analytics age, Valentine's message was largely lost on his critics. Those critics included Tim McCarver, who from the Mets television booth said Valentine goofed in summoning Rojas over left-hander Brian Bohanon. That proclamation came before Rojas' first pitch to O'Neill.

Now it was the following day, with Valentine again looking toward his bullpen in the seventh inning for a reliever to face O'Neill. This time the manager chose lefty Bill Pulsipher, and watched O'Neill deliver an RBI single that extended the Yankees' lead. Valentine glared toward the press level. Then he says he subtly offered a salute with his middle finger.

"I looked up and a couple of the masterminds were looking down and I decided to acknowledge them," Valentine said.

"Nobody understood a platoon differential in those days and I had to explain to the whole world and on WFAN about 18 times that there are right-handers who get left-handers out better than left-handers and nobody believed it, because I didn't have a term for it. If I had a 'platoon differential' or some kind of wonderful nickname I could have given it, everybody would have caught on, but nobody could understand."

The Mets had hired Valentine almost two years earlier largely because he viewed the game differently than most others, especially predecessor Dallas Green. Statistical analysis was still several years away from becoming integrated into the game, but Valentine spoke that language.

"At that time you needed to build with a forward-thinking manager," said Jim Duquette, who spent most of the 1990s working in player development for the Mets and hired Valentine to lead Triple-A Norfolk in 1996. "Dallas Green was old-school, very old-school, and Bobby at the time was at the forefront. Before you had the analytics you were looking for that edge to use every small advantage you had and Bobby saw the game differently in a good way.

"He wasn't afraid to try new things. He was one of the first people that would challenge the establishment. Just because this is how people thought and what the scouts said didn't mean that it was true. He spent a lot of time with video and really helped introduce that to our organization."

Valentine had excelled in three sports at Rippowam High School in Stamford, Connecticut, and was set to accept a football scholarship to USC (as the potential heir apparent to O.J. Simpson at running back) but signed with the Dodgers. Injuries prevented Valentine from reaching his full potential.

Even so, he played 10 major league seasons with the Dodgers, Angels, Padres, Mets, and Mariners. Valentine played his last game at 29 years old and, after coaching in the minor leagues and joining Davey Johnson's staff with the Mets, he became Rangers manager in 1985. His stay in Texas lasted six years, during which the club failed to reach the postseason.

Bobby Valentine brought an analytical mind and street smarts to the Mets dugout, along with flamboyance. He made plenty of friends and enemies along the way.

Valentine spent 1995 in Japan before returning to Norfolk, where he had previously managed one season. In August of 1996, he was summoned from Norfolk to replace Green.

"Bobby was the guy who told the truth to the players, and to me he was great," said Edgardo Alfonzo, who spent 6½ seasons playing for Valentine. "My experience with Bobby was good because he let me play and he trusted me. Now, when you play against Bobby you want to kill him because of the things he does in the dugout, but when you get to know him you understand this guy is for real. He's a real smart guy and he taught me a lot."

Mike Piazza's relationship with Valentine was more complicated. On one hand, Piazza had grown up with the Dodgers, where Tommy Lasorda's colorful personality and idiosyncrasies helped define the organization. Valentine, from his time as a player with the Dodgers, had developed a close relationship with Lasorda, to the point the two considered each other family. So in that sense, the transition should have been seamless for Piazza when he was traded to the Mets during the 1998 season.

Instead, Piazza often found himself frustrated by Valentine's unpredictability and knack for blaming his star catcher.

"If you're that type of personality, then you are going to make some enemies and I think you can't be all things to all people," Piazza said. "I think people are always going to have their supporters and detractors. Tommy [Lasorda] was the same way. A lot of people liked Tommy and a lot of people didn't.

"Sometimes as players we get too comfortable and sometimes you need somebody to shock the system a little bit, even though you might not agree with it. There were times I wanted to kill [Valentine], he would call me out on certain things and I didn't think it was warranted, but nonetheless I had to keep my nose down and just deal with it."

But in an era when big-personality managers still had a place in the game, Valentine certainly fit. Piazza recalled growing up watching managers such as Billy Martin, Sparky Anderson, and Whitey Herzog—in addition to his brother's godfather, Lasorda—preside over successful teams, and there was never a question about who was in charge. It's a stark contrast to the collaboration that has prevailed in recent years, in which front offices have become overwhelmingly involved in scripting the manager's moves and constructing the daily lineup.

Gary Cohen, then a Mets radio broadcaster—he later took his play-by-play talents to television for SNY—ranks Valentine among the great tacticians of the era.

"Bobby V used to say he wished there would be a panel discussion with all the top managers: Jim Leyland, Bobby Cox, and Tony La Russa and all those guys," Cohen said. "That somebody would ask them questions to respond what they would do in a situation. [Valentine] loved that kind of competition between himself and the other managers. In my opinion he probably did know more than anybody else. He sometimes was a little self-defeating in the way he presented it, but he was brilliant as far as being a baseball tactician."

* * *

The Mets began 1998 regarded as a scrappy team built on pitching that could possibly contend in the NL East, and ended the season as a threat. Much of the dynamic changed with a trade orchestrated by general manager Steve Phillips in May that brought Piazza to the Mets. Only eight days earlier the Dodgers, unsuccessful in agreeing to a contract extension with Piazza, had traded the All-Star catcher to the Marlins. To get Piazza from the Marlins, the Mets surrendered prospects Preston Wilson, Ed Yarnall, and Geoff Goetz.

"That '98 team was a real good team, but we felt we were missing a bat," said Duquette, who had ascended to assistant GM under Phillips. "We were a good little team and built around pitching and defense and playing the right way and we had interchangeable parts, but our lineup wasn't deep. That's why the Piazza deal made so much sense for us."

Phillips had upgraded the rotation in February by acquiring veteran left-hander Al Leiter in a trade with the dismantling Marlins, who won the previous World Series. The 32-year-old Leiter had grown up a Mets fan in Toms River, New Jersey, and would be returning to New York after beginning his career with the Yankees.

Leiter received a phone call from Marlins general manager Dave Dombrowski the day before the trade to keep him informed of the possibilities. At the time, Dombrowski was considering offers from the Cardinals and Mets and wanted to know if Leiter had a preference.

"I gave [Dombrowski] the whole story of growing up a Mets fan and lovable losers and my father liked the Mets because they didn't win, and my memories and affinities of going to Shea Stadium with my dad and my brothers," Leiter said. "I told him if he was able to do that for me it would be amazing. He said, 'Look, I hear you and I am glad you told me, but I am going to take the best deal.' Sure enough, the next day Dave told me I was traded to the Mets and I was thrilled."

Piazza's arrival three months later bolstered a lineup that included Alfonzo, John Olerud, Carlos Baerga, and Butch Huskey. The team's biggest power threat to that point, Todd Hundley, was recovering from Tommy John surgery and would be relegated to left field upon his return. Hundley, who had established a franchise record with 41 homers two years earlier, struggled to adapt and was traded to the Dodgers after the season.

Piazza wasn't exactly embraced at Shea Stadium during his early months with the club and regularly heard boos.

"I knew the expectations were high and I knew there was a lot of personal pressure and myself feeling I had to have a good year to warrant a good contract at the end of the season if I was going to be a free agent," Piazza said. "The boos were maybe the fans not feeling like I was going to stay. Maybe I was like a Hessian or a rented soldier and I think there was a lot of times I was pressing. Late in the game I was getting a few hits. I was hitting well average-wise but I wasn't really driving in big runs and I was struggling in the big situations because I was pressing.

"We as athletes have to sort of do things to survive and try to change the energy in a way, so my natural instincts were to sort of go into my shell and I wasn't very approachable. I knew I had to refocus and maybe I wasn't the most friendly guy. And I tell people all the time, when I played you have to do what you have to do to be competitive and I wasn't always the most approachable guy, so maybe with that perception I was being guarded, the fans then said, basically, 'We are just going to let him have it a little bit.'"

For Piazza, the turning point came in the nightcap of a double-header against the Colorado Rockies on August 18 at Shea Stadium. Chuck McElroy had loaded the bases after entering in relief in the seventh, and Piazza smashed a line-drive double to center field that scored all three runs to put the Mets ahead in a 6–3 victory to complete the doubleheader sweep.

"From there I felt the energy turning and I felt after that game the fans started really saying, signs came out, 'One hundred million, a bargain,' type of thing and it was really cool because I think the fans have a unique personality," Piazza said. "The Mets fans are totally unique. They were very much aware at that point if I were playing better there would be demand in the market so then they could have lost me. They traded a couple of good prospects that year when I came from the Marlins, so it was pretty funny. I enjoyed that. I felt it was a trial by fire in a way. It made me better. It made me in a way understand what the dynamics were to play in New York."

The Mets managed to remain in the playoff hunt until the final weekend of the season. But a five-game losing streak to conclude the season, which included getting swept three games in Atlanta on that final weekend, prevented the Mets from reaching the playoffs. Months later, before the start of spring training, Valentine said it was just as well the Mets fell short of October, because his team probably lacked the firepower to compete for a championship. Either Valentine was trying to cushion the disappointment of the near-miss or his intent was to blame the front office for not providing him with enough ammunition.

* * *

From a pure talent standpoint, Valentine's best Mets team was probably the 1999 club. Nelson Doubleday, who then co-owned the team with Fred Wilpon, had prevailed in his push to re-sign Piazza, giving the Mets a foundation around which to build.

The Yankees were on their way to sweeping the Padres, bringing a second World Series title in three seasons to the Bronx. It was during the series Phillips flew to Southern California and finalized a seven-year contract for Piazza worth $91 million. Phillips would admit years later he wasn't sure if there was a Plan B for the Mets if the negotiations with Piazza fizzled.

"We had sort of been looking for that star and hadn't quite found that guy," Phillips said. "We had kicked the tires on Kevin Brown, but we ended up getting Al Leiter. We had considered [Gary] Sheffield back in the time as he was sort of blossoming, but we weren't sure that he was the right fit.

"If not Piazza at that point I am not exactly sure where we would have gone from there because we had given up the prospects to get him, and teams don't like to do that now, but we did it and in the end we felt justified because we re-signed him. It felt like we at least got seven-plus years of Mike and gave him an introduction to the city, which was part of luring him and keeping him there—being a part of what New York could be like and the impact he could have."

Doubleday, who four years later sold his stake in the team to Wilpon amid a bitter divorce between the co-owners, was the clear driving force behind the Piazza contract.

"I think at that point you had some creative tension between two different personalities and like any company, a board room is sometimes going to be contentious or there is going to be disagreement," Piazza said. "But I never detected Fred not wanting to do it. I think it was at a point where they started putting the numbers together and realized it was going to be a big investment and a catcher, true, because it's a risky position—it's like a pitcher, there is a high risk for injury.

"I think Nelson was from that old school like, 'Just get it done,' which was cool. And look, it's something to be celebrated. There is absolutely no way you can downplay his significance to the team and what he did for the team in those days."

Alfonzo had settled in nicely at third base for the previous two seasons, but with Robin Ventura available on the free-agent market, the front office approached him with a request: Would he move to second base? Alfonzo gave his blessing on the position change, giving the team a dynamic infield once Ventura arrived that also included Olerud and Rey Ordonez. The Mets also bolstered their bullpen by adding Armando Benitez, a fireballer with a high upside, in a trade with the Orioles.

"Just like that we started to build something nice," Alfonzo said. "When everybody is coming aboard, now it started to look different— much different than it was before."

The influx of talent didn't translate into a fast start. After the Mets lost a second straight game at Yankee Stadium on June 5, dropping them to 27–28, Phillips fired hitting coach Tom Robson, pitching coach Bob Apodaca, and bullpen coach Randy Niemann. All were strong Valentine allies.

In a circuslike press conference in an auxiliary clubhouse at Yankee Stadium before the series finale, Phillips said he wanted Valentine, who was despondent over the firings, to remain as manager for at least the remainder of the season. In one comical exchange, Barry Stanton of the *Journal News* in Westchester asked why Niemann had been fired given the bullpen was a team strength. Phillips explained he wanted to overhaul all the pitching instructors at once. At the time, Hall of Famer Tom Seaver was serving as a part-time pitching instructor for the team—in addition to his TV analyst duties—leading Stanton to pipe up: "Does this mean Tom Seaver is fired, too?" Valentine, seated next to Phillips, nodded in approval at the question. The answer, of course, was no.

Rickey Henderson, then near the conclusion of his Hall of Fame career, was approached in the clubhouse before the game and asked about hitting coach Robson's firing. In a pure Rickey-like moment, Henderson responded, "Tom Robson? Who dat?"

Valentine put himself on notice, saying if the Mets didn't win somewhere in the neighborhood of 40 games over their next 55 he shouldn't be the manager. The comment was directed toward nemesis Murray Chass of the *New York Times*, who had wondered why Valentine, if so beholden to his coaches, hadn't resigned from his position out of loyalty to them.

"We had stayed up all night talking about it," Valentine said, referring to his coaches. "They wanted me to stick it out, turn it around, and then there was a question about there being 55 games until the trade deadline or something, what was our record going to be? I said it would be 40–15. Luckily, I was able to do the math on the spot without any sleep, a good Stamford public education that is what it will do for you, and son of a gun we won that 40th game and I didn't have to quit."

But the wild press conference at Yankee Stadium in which Valentine put himself on notice wasn't even the wackiest thing to happen that week for the Mets.

Three nights later, Valentine was ejected by plate umpire Randy Marsh for arguing a catcher's interference call against Piazza in the 12th inning of a game against the Blue Jays at Shea Stadium. Upon returning to the clubhouse, Valentine was greeted by Ventura and Orel Hershiser, who goaded him into wearing a disguise and returning to the dugout. Valentine took the stickers that players wear under their eyes to block the sun during day games and formed it into a mustache. He also wore sunglasses and a T-shirt.

As Valentine stood at the end of the tunnel leading to the dugout, he was spotted by the third-base camera and outed on the Mets' television broadcast. Valentine later jokingly blamed Hershiser for not shielding him, as the two had pre-arranged. The penalty for Valentine was a two-game suspension and $5,000 fine.

"Things were crazy then—they were really crazy, that '99," Valentine said. "Every day was like sniper fire. You had to watch what mine you might step on, but I got suspended three games and I asked [NL president] Leonard Coleman if it could get down to two games, and he reduced it. Then I begged them not to start it immediately, because I didn't want to miss the home games. And [Coleman] let me serve it on the road."

Pat Mahomes (whose son Patrick would become a NFL star and Super Bowl–champion quarterback for the Kansas City Chiefs) was the winning pitcher in relief on July 30 against the Cubs at Wrigley Field, moving the Mets atop the NL East for the first time since April. The Mets' lead was 1½ games a week later, after they had won for the 40th time in the 55-game stretch, backing Valentine's wild prediction.

Any dreams of a division title were dashed by a seven-game September losing streak that pushed the Mets clearly in the Braves' rearview mirror. The wild card was still a possibility, and the Mets' three-game sweep of the Pirates on the final weekend of the regular season allowed Valentine's crew to finish tied with the Reds for that berth. The winning run in the finale against the Pirates scored on a Brad Clontz wild pitch.

"There was so much to that season and just the fact they hadn't been to the postseason in 11 years made that year incredibly special for me,"

Mike Piazza was the missing piece to the Mets' lineup in the late 1990s. His bat helped the team win the NL pennant in 2000, leading to the first Subway World Series in 44 years. (Jed Jacobsohn/ALLSPORT)

Gary Cohen said. "I started in '89, I got there right after this great wave of success, so I had never done a postseason game, so all of a sudden that year happens and it was my favorite year by far.

"I have this vision of Piazza standing at home plate after the winning run scored, with a bat still in his hand and not knowing what to do with himself because he was supposed to drive in the run. Instead, Clontz comes in and the first pitch bounces up on the screen and the Mets win the game. Piazza is bewildered. He's not even celebrating with the team. He's got the bat in his hand, waiting for whatever was supposed to happen."

MLB adopted a postseason format beginning in 2012 in which two wild-card winners in each league began playing one game to determine who would advance to the division series. An iteration of this format was Mets-Reds on October 4, 1999.

Al Leiter was unsure as he left Shea Stadium a day earlier whether he would be facing the Diamondbacks in Game 1 of the NLDS or the Reds in the one-game playoff. A rain delay in Milwaukee had kept the Mets wondering whether the Reds would win to force the tiebreaker. The Mets waited on the tarmac at LaGuardia airport for an indication before taking off for Cincinnati.

Leiter had plenty of big-game experience on his resume after pitching in the World Series for the Blue Jays and Marlins, but that history couldn't have prepared him for what awaited at Cinergy Field as he began throwing in the bullpen.

"Warming up at that stadium was amazing, it was loud as shit, it was a Monday night game, every college kid I think from within 50 miles of that place, they were there in rare form," Leiter said. "They were lined up down the line right where you warm up, and they were in my face and they were definitely loud and there was no filter in what they were saying to me.

"In some weird way if you yelled at me it got me more focused, and I was one of those guys that pitched angry and if you pissed me off it helped me. I wanted to feel angry. I wanted to feel like the batter is taking food off my table and wants to hurt me, and I want to hurt you. I am a little crazy, but I believe that. These kids were crazy so everybody was already drunk and feeling lubricated. It was intense."

In Mets lore this became the Al Leiter game. Leiter scuffled through a season in which his ERA surged above four, but on this night he was every bit the ace the Mets needed. The tone for the night was set in the first inning, when Alfonzo cleared the center-field fence against Steve Parris after Henderson had singled leading off the game. Leiter had all the support he needed.

"What I really remember was Al coming off the field in the first inning and I never saw him so amped up," Valentine said. "He was always kicking and spitting and pounding his glove after every call, but in that first inning he was a 2.0 version of Al on adrenaline and then when he got out of the first inning and we had the lead it was like, 'Katy, bar the door.' There was no looking back. There was no question."

Jeffrey Hammonds singled in the second inning, and the Reds didn't get another hit until the ninth, when Pokey Reese doubled leading off. Leiter would escape that to finish with a two-hit shutout in the Mets' 5–0 victory that sent them to the postseason for the first time since 1988.

"It was one of my favorite games I ever caught, and we clicked that night," Piazza said. "Every time he shook me off it was like we were just trying to shake for the sake of it, we were so locked in. As a catcher for me, that is the one thing I really enjoyed about my job: I didn't have to go out and hit a three-run home run all the time. If I caught a shutout like that, a great game like that, that was just as good. That was one of my favorite games, no question."

For Valentine, who had managed 1,704 major league games with the Rangers and Mets without reaching the postseason, the postgame celebration resonated the loudest. The previous month, after a tough loss in Philadelphia, Valentine had suggested he didn't deserve to continue as manager if the Mets missed the playoffs.

The next stop was Arizona, for a NLDS game that wouldn't start until after 11 PM, on the east coast because for the first time since the Mets' inception, both New York teams had reached the postseason. As the Yankees began their ALDS against the Rangers, hours before the Mets played, the buzz was real that New York could be headed toward a first Subway World Series since 1956.

Alfonzo, in a repeat of his Cincinnati heroics, homered against Randy Johnson in the first inning of Game 1. But his truly magical moment came in the ninth, when he blasted a tie-breaking grand slam against Bobby Chouinard.

"That game was so exciting," Alfonzo said. "It was like, 'Come on, we need to beat Randy Johnson because he's their ace.' The count went to 3–1 against Chouinard in the ninth and I knew he didn't want to walk me. I got a good swing—sometimes you know what is coming but miss the ball—and it was an amazing feeling. I was around the bases and it was a dream. It was like, 'Wow, I did it.'"

Todd Stottlemyre beat Kenny Rogers the following night sending the series tied to Shea Stadium. In Game 3, the Mets jumped on Arizona's bullpen and scored six runs in the sixth inning in rolling to a 9–2 victory. Notably, Piazza was on the bench for that game because of a bruised left thumb. And Piazza would remain on the bench the following day as the Mets attempted to clinch the series.

"Most unbelievable thing, because once again, 'What, Mike is not going to play?'" Valentine said. "It's the biggest game the Mets have played in 11 years and Mike's not playing? That was something, but he had the bruised thumb and he just couldn't catch. He could catch the ball on the outside for a right-hander, but he couldn't move and get that one on the inside, especially a sinker or Leiter's cutter."

Piazza, who had received an injection that further inflamed the thumb, was crawling to the finish line of the season at a time the Mets needed him to sprint.

"It's frustrating as an athlete because you get to that point and I obviously had a good season production-wise but I had played so much that I was getting to the end and these nagging injuries were starting to mount a little bit," Piazza said.

His absence left the catching duties to Todd Pratt, a 32-year-old career backup who had 16 homers over seven seasons in the major leagues.

With it 3–3 in the 10th inning, Pratt batted against Matt Mantei and lofted a flyball to center field on which Steve Finley had a beat. The ball carried Finley to the fence, where he leaped and appeared to have it in his glove. Except the ball was behind the fence. Game over. The Mets were headed to the NLCS.

"I still think Finley caught the ball, but wanted to get on the plane, didn't want to play anymore, because I see a lot of guys go up against the fence and come down and I always knew when they caught it and I was sure he caught that ball," Valentine said.

Cohen had the call on WFAN radio and hesitated—as had Pratt rounding first base—as Finley approached the center-field fence.

"We had seen Finley make catches like that so many times," Cohen said. "But at Shea in those days where he tried to catch it was right near the gate that opened for the batting cages and there was a little bit of a depression right in front of the fence and I think when he went to plant to make his jump he hit that depression and that is why his back kind of went into the fence instead of elevating a little further and I think that was the difference between him catching and not catching it.

"But when he first went up for it I had no idea whether he caught it or not, and then he came down and you could just see from the way he hung his head that he hadn't caught it. Pratt saw the same thing and we both hesitated and then both reacted."

The lingering memory to Alfonzo was the manner in which the old ballpark shook—maybe more violently than it had at any point over the last 13 years, since Bill Buckner misplayed Mookie Wilson's grounder into an improbable Mets victory over the Red Sox in Game 6 of the World Series.

"Shea Stadium was bumping," Alfonzo said. "People were jumping and you could feel it. You could feel the whole stadium moving. That was a great feeling for us, the players, giving Mets fans an opportunity a playoff series victory, especially since it had been a long time since they had done it."

The reward was to face the nemesis Braves, who had owned the Mets for the latter portion of the decade. Chipper Jones was Public Enemy

No. 1, but Greg Maddux, John Smoltz, and Tom Glavine weren't far behind. During that regular season, the Mets had finished 3–9 against the Braves.

But the Leiter gem in Cincinnati and Pratt's home run against the Diamondbacks had the Mets feeling like a team of destiny.

"I really thought that team was going to win the whole thing," Valentine said. "We had a good team. But there was that stumbling block, it was the Braves. It was tough. Every year that Braves team was there. They had those position players and the stability of the team and they would always bring in somebody. Brian Jordan came in and then a left-handed starter came in and then the next left-handed starter and then John Rocker and then that left-hander we could never hit, Mike Remlinger. He pitched in the minor leagues for me before I went to Japan. I came back and he was a star."

The first three games of the NLCS were all close, with the Braves prevailing. Maybe the biggest heartbreaker was Game 3, in which the Braves scored an unearned run against Leiter in the first inning and won 1–0, behind the combined shutout of Glavine, Remlinger, and Rocker.

But the Mets avoided a sweep with a 3–2 victory in Game 4 before going to the 15th inning the following night. Ventura delivered what should have been the ultimate, a walk-off grand slam, but officially it became a game-winning single, as he was mobbed by teammates and never reached second base.

"That was one of the most epic games I had ever seen or ever called," Cohen said. "Just the fact it was raining throughout the game and just all the maneuvering with Valentine and Bobby Cox."

The series, still very much alive, returned to Atlanta, where Leiter got the ball on three days' rest. In the previous game he had been warming up in the bullpen and ready to enter before Ventura cleared the fence. But Leiter was flat in this Game 6 start and got knocked out in the first inning, burying the Mets in a 5–0 hole. The Mets somehow rallied to tie the game at 7–7 in the seventh on Piazza's two-run homer against John Smoltz.

"My solace in the whole thing, when Piazza hit the game-tying home run, we tied it up and then I felt like, 'Yes, I sucked, but frig, the game is tied up in the seventh,'" Leiter said.

The Mets took the lead in the eighth before John Franco allowed a game-tying single to Brian Hunter. In the 10th the Mets went ahead against Rocker, but Benitez blew the save in the bottom of the inning. The game was decided in the 11th with Kenny Rogers issuing a bases-loaded walk to Andruw Jones that gave the Braves a 10–9 victory.

"I am telling you, if we win that game we go to the World Series," Leiter said. "We win Game 7, without a doubt in my mind."

* * *

In the summer of 2000, Valentine's hometown of Stamford, Connecticut, had two favorite sons in the spotlight. In the sporting arena there was Valentine, who still maintained roots in the city—he owned a popular downtown sports bar "Bobby V's" where the locals would converge to watch one of their own manage the Mets and then maybe on an off day find him greeting guests at the bar. In the political arena there was Stamford High graduate Joseph Lieberman, a U.S. senator from Connecticut who had just been selected as Al Gore's running mate for the upcoming presidential election.

As much as Valentine, as a proud Stamford native, might have liked Lieberman, he had his own loyalties in this election: George W. Bush, the Republican candidate for president, had been the Rangers' managing partner during Valentine's managerial tenure with the team. The two remained friends after Bush fired Valentine and even worked out together in Pittsburgh, where Bush was campaigning when the Mets were in town in 2000.

The Mets were a threat that year to reach the playoffs again, leading me to ask Valentine in a column for the *Connecticut Post* who was the bigger deal in Stamford, him or Lieberman. Valentine provided a concise response that resonated louder as summer turned to fall: "We'll see in November which of us wins," Valentine quipped.

Much of the same Mets team that had lost to the Braves in the NLCS had returned for 2000, with a notable exception: Olerud departed through free agency to sign with the Mariners. The Mets signed Todd Zeile as his replacement at first base, and boosted the rotation by trading for Mike Hampton, who had finished 22–4 with a 2.90 ERA for the Astros the previous year. In the deal the Mets also acquired outfielder Derek Bell, surrendering Roger Cedeno and Octavio Dotel.

"I think the '99 team was better, but in 2000 we had guys that really had energy and hunger to win, play hard," Alfonzo said.

Well, almost everybody played hard. Rickey Henderson continued marching to his own beat and was released in May, a day after he posed in the batter's box and watched a shot to left field bang off the fence at Shea Stadium. Henderson got as far as first base. His departure from the scene left Valentine to juggle an outfield of Bell, Jay Payton, Timo Perez, and Benny Agbayani.

"We felt like we were going to win with pitching and defense, and Shea was a hard place to hit," Jim Duquette said. "We wanted to make sure we had good overall hitters, so that is where Bobby did his best magic. He matched up guys and put them in situations where they could succeed. He got a lot out of the outfield.

"The top part of the lineup could compete with anyone. The second half of the lineup wasn't as strong, and that is where they really needed the manager to figure out what the matchups looked like that particular night. And that's where Bobby was magic."

In a historic event, the Yankees and Mets played a two-ballpark doubleheader on July 8. In the afternoon game, at Shea Stadium, Dwight

Gooden returned to the Yankees for one last hurrah and beat the team for which he had starred in the 1980s. One might have thought that would be the storyline for the day.

But it was the nightcap, across town at Yankee Stadium, for which the day is remembered. Piazza, batting in the second inning, was drilled in the helmet by a Roger Clemens fastball and dropped at home plate, departing with a concussion. To the Mets the beaning seemed suspicious, given Piazza's success against Clemens in recent seasons. Piazza had homered in his previous three games against Clemens.

In the trainer's room in the visitor's clubhouse at Yankee Stadium, Piazza was still trying to gain his bearings when the Yankees' team physician, Dr. Stuart Hershon, entered and told him Clemens was on the phone and wanted to speak with him.

Piazza responded, "Tell him to go fuck himself."

Forgiveness clearly wasn't on Piazza's mind at that point.

"I would expect at that point to be brushed off the plate, but I didn't expect to almost have my head taken off," Piazza said. "And I think maybe [Clemens] had realized in his frustration that he was kind of like the kid that broke the window. You're doing something and then 'Oh, shit, what I did just do?' And that is why he felt a remorse to try to call me."

Rey Ordonez's broken arm left the Mets in need of a shortstop, and Phillips filled the need with a trade that sent Melvin Mora and three minor leaguers to the Orioles for Mike Bordick. The veteran Bordick stabilized the position after Kurt Abbott had failed to play at a satisfactory level.

The Mets finished the season with 94 victories, good enough for a second straight National League wild card berth. For the first time in franchise history the Mets had qualified for the postseason in consecutive seasons.

The Mets' victory over the Giants in the NLDS was highlighted by Bobby Jones' brilliance in Game 4. In one of the best-pitched games in franchise history, Jones surrendered only a fifth-inning double to Jeff Kent and finished with a one-hitter. Jones retired the side in order in eight of the nine innings.

"When you consider the gravity of the situation, Leiter in '99, the one-game playoff against the Reds, he pitched a fantastic game, but you don't think about Bobby Jones as somebody who is going to pitch that type of a game," Cohen said. "He was a steady middle of the rotation kind of guy, but to go out there and throw a one-hitter in a clinching game, that ranks up there in the top-five best pitching performances in Mets history when you consider the situation."

Unlike the previous year, the Braves wouldn't be around to torment the Mets in the NLCS. The Cardinals swept the defending NL champions in the NLDS, leaving the Mets with an easier path, at least psychologically, in attempting to reach their first World Series in 14 years.

The Cardinals were no match for the Mets in a NLCS best remembered for Rick Ankiel's meltdown in which he lost all sense of the strike zone, effectively ending his pitching career. The left-hander had walked six batters in 2⅔ innings against the Braves in the NLDS. Given another opportunity, he walked five batters in 1⅓ innings against the Mets. Ankiel returned to the game as an outfielder, which included 20 games played for the Mets at the conclusion of his career.

The romp over the Cardinals in five games left the Mets to await the conclusion of the Yankees-Mariners ALCS to find out their World Series opponent.

"That NLCS is the first time I can remember the ballpark shaking in a way that scared me," Cohen said. "You could feel the mezzanine above us swaying back and forth and I don't recall having felt that in all the years I had been calling the games, because we sat right below the mezzanine, but it struck me during that Cardinals series. The Mets did a lot of bashing in that series, so there was a lot of things for fans to celebrate and it reached a crescendo that I don't think it ever reached in the World Series."

* * *

Months before the 20th anniversary of the historic Subway World Series between the New York City rivals, Mike Piazza sat with me in the media room at the Mets spring-training complex and tried to make sense of what had occurred in Game 2.

Piazza, in all the time that had passed since then, still hadn't received an explanation from Roger Clemens about what happened that night at Yankee Stadium.

It was Clemens' first time facing Piazza since the beaning three months earlier. On a 1-2 pitch, Clemens jammed Piazza with a fastball, breaking the bat and sending the barrel toward the mound. Piazza, unsure about the locale of the ball—it had squibbed foul to the right side—started toward first base and was startled to find the barrel of the bat headed in his direction. Clemens had fielded the shard and fired it toward his nemesis. Both benches emptied, but order was restored without punches thrown.

"A lot of people come up to me today and say, 'You should have kicked Roger's ass,'" Piazza said. "Easy for them to say. I hit a home run off Jeff Nelson that game, which I never would have done if I fought Clemens. Maybe he would have beat me up, maybe I would have beat him up, who knows? When you get two big guys and you are rolling around, who knows? And look, I don't think anybody really wants to see that during the World Series."

Piazza's best guess is the buildup to the showdown between the two future Hall of Famers raised Clemens' adrenaline level in a super-charged environment.

"Personally, I have always had a good ability to stay calm in those moments," Piazza said. "I think it's one of my attributes that helped me, but some guys and obviously in his case maybe the excitement and buildup was difficult to handle."

Clemens later tried to say he thought Piazza's bat fragment was the ball.

"Until this day I don't know what the hell happened there," said Alfonzo, who was among the first Mets onto the field when the benches emptied. "Roger Clemens says, 'I thought it was the ball.' Come on, man…. Mike is a guy who is really calm and really a gentleman. If it had been someone other than Mike, I don't know if he wouldn't have charged the mound."

Even with Piazza's homer in the ninth against Nelson, the Yankees won 6–5 to give them the first two games of the series. The Mets' loss the previous night in Game 1 had been more painful for them.

In a scoreless game with two outs in the sixth inning, Todd Zeile hit a shot to deep left field against Andy Pettitte that seemed destined for the seats and a two-run homer. Timo Perez, on first base, thought the ball was out and slowed down running. The ball ended up in play, with Perez thrown out at the plate on Zeile's double.

The Mets took a 3–2 lead into the ninth inning and were within two outs of the victory when Paul O'Neill walked against Benitez to complete a 10-pitch at-bat. Benitez allowed singles to Luis Polonia and Jose Vizcaino that loaded the bases before Chuck Knoblauch hit a sacrifice fly that tied it. The Yankees won in the 12th inning on Vizcaino's RBI single against Turk Wendell.

Benitez had been electric during the regular season, but his Mets career is largely defined by the big games in which he flopped. None was bigger than Game 1 of the Subway Series.

"Unfortunately closers, even Trevor Hoffman had to go through this in a way, as much as you are remembered for the closing, you are also going to be remembered for the games you don't close," Piazza said. "I don't think it's deserved, but unfortunately that is just the way it is in sports and the way we review and report sports. If it wasn't for Benitez we wouldn't have been there. He was dominating the whole year and really pitched his ass off the whole year. It was a situation, at times unfortunately he didn't get it done and it would have been one of those times that he could have changed the course of the series."

The Yankees, with a nucleus that included Derek Jeter, Bernie Williams, Tino Martinez, Jorge Posada, and Mariano Rivera, extended their World Series winning streak to 14 straight games with their victories against the Mets in the Bronx. The streak had started in the 1996 World Series, when the Yankees fell into an 0–2 deficit against the Braves and then rallied to win the next four games. Sweeps of the Padres ('98) and Braves ('99) ensued.

But on the surface there appeared to be a vulnerability about these 2000 Yankees. The team had struggled in the final month and finished with only 87 victories, as starting pitchers David Cone, Orlando "El Duque" Hernandez, and trade-deadline addition Denny Neagle endured subpar seasons. The Mets had every reason to believe their crosstown rival was beatable, but also respected the Yankees' winning pedigree.

"It's kind of like in your house when you are 12 and your brother who is 16 can kick your ass because he is four years older and that is like dog years and he's a man and you have no shot," Leiter said. "And then that same big brother is now 34 and you are 30 and you are every bit as big in muscles and you know you can take him, but there is still that hesitancy. It's like, 'I'm supposed to be able to kick his ass.' I didn't feel like we were inferior and we didn't belong, but it was the Yankees and their championships and the lore and Yankee Stadium and all the Yankee bullshit. There was a little bit of that, I would say."

Agbayani's RBI double against Hernandez in the eighth inning of Game 3 gave the Mets a 3–2 lead, with another run scoring later, and Benitez got the final three outs to give the Mets oxygen. But that momentum was short-lived: Jeter homered on Bobby Jones' first pitch of the game the following night, and the Mets' bats went silent against Neagle and the Yankees' bullpen in a 3–2 loss.

Now it was on Leiter to keep the Mets' season alive. The pitcher counted Bruce Springsteen among his friends and was told before Game 5 that the "The Boss" planned to helicopter in to watch in person. Leiter during batting practice even walked over to the VIP seats behind home plate to find out where Springsteen would be sitting.

Leiter battled through eight innings, allowing only solo homers to Williams and Jeter, and then made it clear he wanted the ball for the ninth in a 2–2 game.

"I knew it was my last start until we go down to Port St. Lucie the next year," Leiter said. "And [pitching coach] Dave Wallace came to me down at the end of the dugout at Shea asking me how I feel and I screamed real loud that I wanted to stay in and said some curse words, and I said it loud enough just so Valentine could hear it over at the bat rack at the other end of the dugout, and it worked."

Valentine's faith in his pitcher was rewarded when Leiter began the inning by striking out Martinez and O'Neill. But Posada drew a full-count walk and Scott Brosius singled, before Luis Sojo hit a dribbler through the middle on Leiter's 142nd pitch of the night. Two runs scored on the play, as Jay Payton's throw home bounced away from Piazza for an error.

The Mets tried to rally against Rivera, getting a walk from Agbayani before Piazza hit a shot to center with two outs that seemed destined to depart the ballpark. The ball died in Williams' glove. The Yankees had their three-peat.

"The only good part about it was to give Joe Torre a little bit of a heart attack before the celebration," Piazza said. "It wasn't like I struck out and they went, 'Yeah!' It was like a 'Uhhh-ahhh,' type of thing. I did take a bit of miniscule pride in that."

On a clear night the ball might have carried out, but the overcast and mist didn't help. Leiter remembers those conditions perfectly because after the game he learned it was the reason Springsteen decided not to attend; helicopter travel would have been risky. Leiter was too preoccupied during the game to notice Springsteen's absence.

"I never got as emotional in any game that I ever pitched than that game," Leiter said. "It was physically and mentally and emotionally draining."

The Mets front office understood exactly what kind of opportunity had escaped the organization.

"It was the closest five-game World Series, it felt like, ever," Steve Phillips said. "Who knows if we get Game 1 what happens? We had it in our grasp and it got away from us—Timo and certainly late in the game from the bullpen. But if we win Game 1 you wonder what happens and certainly I do, and if Piazza, it certainly looked like he got that ball in Game 5, the drive to center field and for whatever reason it petered out.

"I think we all look back with what ifs, but in the moment as a general manager it's really not enjoyable going through the playoffs and the World Series. It's literally physical pain when you go through it because you hang on every pitch."

The series was bittersweet for Piazza, and not only because it marked the only World Series appearance of his Hall of Fame career.

"People still talk about Clemens and the bat," Piazza said. "I think society today, we don't differentiate between famous and infamous all the time. It is one of those things in my career that is frustrating because my one World Series event, it's the Subway Series, it's a historic series.

"We had a lot of great games against the Yankees in '99 and 2000 and I get remembered for almost having my head taken off and then having a bat thrown at me. And maybe if we had found a way to win the World Series it would have alleviated that tension as well."

* * *

Alex Rodriguez was regarded as the best all-around player in baseball, coming off a season in which he hit 41 homers for the Mariners in helping them reach the ALCS. Still only 25 years old and represented by superagent Scott Boras, the rightful expectation was the star shortstop would receive the richest contract in baseball history as he arrived at free agency following the 2000 season.

The Yankees had the homegrown icon Jeter entrenched at shortstop, leaving them unlikely to seriously pursue Rodriguez at a time A-Rod shifting to third base wasn't a consideration. If Rodriguez was going to play in New York, it would have to be for the Mets, for whom he had rooted growing up in Miami. Rodriguez's favorite player was Keith Hernandez.

Steve Phillips and Boras convened at the GM Meetings, where contract parameters were discussed. A week later Phillips announced the Mets had no interest in pursuing Rodriguez, citing the potential "24-plus-1" environment it would have created in the clubhouse, as the shortstop sought amenities such as office space at Shea Stadium and a tent in which his merchandise could be sold.

"Are you kidding me?" Jim Duquette said. "Can you imagine that then or now? It just wouldn't happen. We barely had enough office space for the people who worked there. We are going to try to carve out another office out for Alex Rodriguez or any player? We all know how big the clubhouse was there at Shea, it was pretty tiny."

The idea of a circus coming to Queens was unappealing to Phillips—never mind that he would have had to convince Doubleday and Wilpon to spend a huge sum for a second time in three offseasons.

"I had Mike Piazza, who was our biggest star, the most low-maintenance star ever," Phillips said in an interview with ESPN New York radio in 2018. "There was no entourage, no strength coach, no hitting coach. There was just Mike Piazza, baseball player. I was like, 'How am I going to manage this, with Alex and all this other stuff, and Mike being a baseball player?'"

Rodriguez received a 10-year contract worth a record $252 million from the Rangers. Three years into that deal he was traded to the Yankees—and shifted to third base—after Aaron Boone tore the anterior cruciate ligament in his left knee during an offseason basketball game. Rodriguez spent the remainder of his controversial career with the Yankees, which included a one-year suspension in 2014 for his involvement with Biogenesis, a lab that provided players with banned performance enhancing drugs. But Rodriguez's legacy also included helping the Yankees win the World Series in 2009, the highlight of a career in which he hit 696 homers and won three MVP awards.

In his second baseball life, as a TV analyst, Rodriguez suggested on ESPN he might have left more than $100 million on the table to sign with the Mets if they had extended him such an offer following the 2000 season. Duquette scoffs at such a notion.

"Boras signed an unbelievable deal for him," Duquette said. "He was going to sign for $130 million less to play for the team that was his childhood dream because he loved Keith Hernandez? Listen, we all love Keith Hernandez, but are you going to give up $130 million? Come on."

Rey Ordonez remained the Mets shortstop, leaving Piazza as the marquee attraction in the lineup. The front office instead focused on finding rotation help, after Mike Hampton—citing the superior Colorado school system—departed for the Rockies, who gave him an eight-year contract worth $121 million.

"Our feeling was we didn't need to get a whole lot better, we just needed to keep signing our pitchers and we made that run at Hampton because he became a free agent," Duquette said. "Then we lost out to him because of the better school system in Colorado. We signed Kevin Appier, who was the next best guy that year among the starting pitchers, and it precipitated our declining years."

* * *

The phone in Piazza's hotel room rang around 9 AM on a Tuesday in Pittsburgh late in the 2001 season. The Mets were off the previous night after concluding a series in Miami on Sunday, and Piazza had joined a group of friends in watching the Broncos play the Giants on *Monday Night Football*. Piazza now heard a despondent voice on the other end of the phone. It was his agent Dan Lozano, who had been out with Piazza the night before. "They got us, man. They got us," Lozano muttered into the phone. Piazza, confused, was told to turn on the TV. The North Tower of the World Trade Center was smoldering, and within minutes a second plane hit, this time striking the South Tower.

"I just couldn't believe it was real," Piazza said.

Leiter, scheduled to pitch that night, had departed his teammates after the series in Miami—he came home to accompany his young daughter to her first day of school in Manhattan—and was on a plane taxiing the runway at LaGuardia airport for his flight to Pittsburgh when the pilot informed passengers there would be a delay because of reports a "news helicopter" had struck the World Trade Center. Within minutes, Leiter was told his flight was canceled and the airport closed.

His mind racing—after all, he had a game to pitch in Pittsburgh that night—Leiter ran through the airport and found a taxi out front, telling the driver he needed to get to Philadelphia, where he planned to get another flight.

Somewhere in New Jersey, Leiter began hearing reports on the radio of additional plane crashes and realized America was under attack. He called the team's director of media relations, Jay Horwitz, and said he was turning back.

"It was obvious there was no way we would be playing that night," Leiter said.

In all, four commercial airliners were used as weapons against the United States on 9/11. Two caused the implosion of the North and South Towers of the World Trade Center, killing 2,606 people. Another hit the Pentagon, and a fourth plane crashed in western Pennsylvania after heroic passengers had stormed the cockpit and overtaken the hijackers.

The Mets, staying near a federal building in downtown Pittsburgh, were ordered to evacuate their hotel. The team was taken to the outskirts of the city and awaited further instructions.

Leiter, in the taxi cab in New Jersey, discovered he wouldn't be allowed back into Manhattan, as all passageways to the island had been closed. Unsure where to go, he called Yankees broadcaster Michael Kay, a longtime friend, and asked if he could come to Kay's condo in Westchester. The two spent the afternoon watching the news coverage. By nightfall, trains were running back to Manhattan, and Leiter railed to Grand Central Station before hiking home 42 blocks, with his path virtually desolate, except for the occasional emergency vehicle racing past him with the siren blaring.

"It was eerie," Leiter said.

Baseball was on hold indefinitely, with Commissioner Bud Selig's announcement that all games had been postponed. With it evident their series in Pittsburgh wouldn't happen, the Mets bussed home.

"Two busses to New York and when you crossed the George Washington Bridge you saw the smoke coming out of Ground Zero," Alfonzo said. "That was devastating."

In an emotional meeting at Shea Stadium, team owners Nelson Doubleday and Fred Wilpon addressed the players. Like many in the room, the Mets owners had friends who were missing in the World Trade Center.

"Nelson came in and was very emotional and cried and was very sad," Piazza said. "The message obviously was we're not going to be playing for a little while, let's...whatever you guys want to do. Everybody was like, 'If you want to be involved, be involved.'"

With Valentine taking the lead, the Mets turned Shea Stadium into a supply center and tried to boost morale throughout the city, whether that meant visits with firefighters, police officers, or rescue workers. Piazza visited hospitals. Valentine, who had lost friends in the towers, was non-stop energy, trying to comfort whomever he could.

"Nine-eleven took a lot out of me," Valentine said. "If I had someone smart that I could sit in a room with back then and they could tell me what was going on, they probably would have said I had a bout of depression. That's what I think it was. There was so much to do and I felt right from the start, those first five days, I thought we were going to be pulling survivors out of that rubble by the hour and they were going to have flatbed trucks trying to move them to hospitals. We didn't pull out one person. There wasn't one person saved during five days of the most miserable mourning."

The season resumed on September 17, with the Mets returning to Pittsburgh for the three-game series that was postponed the previous week. The Mets were 71–73 and eight games removed from first place in the NL East.

The aftermath of the pennant-winning season and Subway Series had been a grind for Valentine's crew, which failed to offset Hampton's departure, receiving underwhelming seasons from Steve Trachsel, Glendon Rusch, and Bruce Chen.

But the disappointment of a lost season almost seemed like an afterthought following the 9/11 attacks.

"When the season started back up I felt so physically drained, but I also felt like that I failed," Valentine said. "I was around such misery. I was going to funerals. I just did too much stuff. I was trying to do the right thing and I just think I did the wrong thing because I didn't combat it real well.

"I was different—angry, too. I really had the thought of enlisting and thinking I could do something to combat the evil that was out there. Not going to the front line, but I thought maybe I could lead some men in the right way because those were weird times. With George the president,

I really cared for that guy. He was a good guy. He always treated me so darn well and he got put in that no-win situation. I was feeling for him, wanting to do something, knowing that probably whatever you do is going to turn out wrong."

The Mets swept the three games in Pittsburgh and returned home for the first sporting event in New York City since the terrorist attacks.

"I was glad it was us and not the Yankees," Leiter said.

In an electric pregame ceremony, with the Mets wearing FDNY and NYPD caps that had become part of their uniform, bagpipes played as American flags waved throughout the stands and Diana Ross performed "God Bless America" and Marc Anthony the national anthem. A crowd of 41,235 had come to Shea Stadium to bring a sense of normalcy back to the city, even as rescue workers were still sifting through debris in lower Manhattan. That the nemesis Braves were the opponent really didn't seem to matter. The Mets were at home playing baseball again.

"When you walked to the field and saw and heard all the fans there and 'U-S-A, U-S-A,' that was emotion," Alfonzo said. "You feel sad and at the same time you are going to play."

Piazza recalled just wanting to survive the night without breaking down emotionally.

"And for me emotionally when the tribute with the bagpipes, when I hear bagpipes I get emotional even now," Piazza said. "I go to Scotland every year and they have the bagpipers there and they play 'Scotland the Brave' and it's a wonderful instrument. It evokes and draws out emotions, so when I hear that coming in I started just tearing up.

"We as athletes wanted to be strong and be a positive example, but at that point I started praying and I said many times, 'Please, let me get through the night.' I didn't care if I got a hit—obviously you don't want to embarrass yourself as an athlete, but as the game went on, then you are back to your familiar surroundings and naturally your instincts take over."

Liza Minnelli's rendition of "New York, New York" during the seventh inning stretch added to the night's pageantry.

Chen allowed an unearned run over seven innings and departed with it 1–1. In the eighth, John Franco allowed two base runners and was replaced by Armando Benitez, who surrendered a RBI double to Brian Jordan.

Steve Karsay, a Queens native who had attended Christ the King High School, was summoned from the Braves' bullpen to protect a 2–1 lead. The right-hander Karsay was among the best setup men in baseball that season and entered with a 1.64 ERA.

Matt Lawton grounded out to begin the eighth, before Karsay worked a full count to Alfonzo, who admits he was thinking throughout the at-bat of trying to hit a game-tying homer. Alfonzo drew a walk, bringing up Piazza, who took a first-pitch fastball for a strike.

"I do remember that distinctly when I took the first pitch and I said to myself, 'Shit, this is probably the best pitch I am going to get,'" Piazza said.

Karsay followed with a fastball, and Piazza clobbered it to the deepest reaches of Shea Stadium. The call belonged to Howie Rose in the Mets television booth.

"And it's hit deep to left-center, Andruw Jones on the run…this one has a chance…home run!" Rose said. "And the Mets lead 3–2."

Piazza took a curtain call. Baseball was back in New York and the Mets had a win. Piazza will forever be linked to the healing that began for New York after 9/11 and appreciates that place in history.

Players grow up dreaming of hitting a home run to win the World Series, but a jolt to bring back a city taps different emotions.

"I just thank God every day that I was in that position," Piazza said. "It's a different type of home run. At times it's frustrating too because I hear the stories that people tell to me and the pain comes back. I have heard some powerful stories about people that were lost, but on the same note it is inspiring and it's an honor for me that people put that home run and that moment in a very high place."

CHAPTER 2
VALENTINE'S DAY MASSACRE

Bobby Valentine is convinced an incident involving the owner's son cost him his job as Mets manager.

To be fair, the 2002 season was disastrous all around for the Mets, who finished last in the NL East after general manager Steve Phillips' gamble on aging players the previous winter backfired.

Phillips had traded for Mo Vaughn, Roberto Alomar, and Jeromy Burnitz and added Roger Cedeno through free agency. On paper the Mets lineup was loaded—the returning cast included Mike Piazza and Edgardo Alfonzo—but the anticipated fireworks show at Shea Stadium never materialized. All four of the lineup additions had disappointed, none more so than Alomar, whose Hall of Fame career entered rapid decline.

Valentine had been on the job for six-plus seasons and often feuded with Phillips, suggesting a managerial change was possible. But as this 75-win debacle was about to conclude, Valentine says owner Fred Wilpon told him his job was safe.

Wilpon was grooming his son Jeff to become involved in the organization and asked a favor of Valentine as the manager prepared to hold a season-ending meeting with his coaches: Could Jeff Wilpon sit in on the meeting? Fred Wilpon wanted his son immersed in all aspects of the organization and told Valentine not to worry about disruption, as Jeff Wilpon would be there to listen and not talk. As Valentine recalls, the elder Wilpon insisted that Jeff Wilpon would not speak up for two years. The plan was for his son to be seen, but not heard. Valentine was fine with the arrangement.

Tom Robson, the team's bench coach, had been a respected hitting coach with the Mets previously. During the coaches' meeting, Robson began speaking about the team's hitting woes, prompting Jeff Wilpon to violate his gag order. Wilpon insisted that Robson's analysis was amiss, and began interjecting his own thoughts on hitting philosophy. Wilpon cited the swing instruction he had received from some of the country's best golf professionals, whose teachings differed from what Robson was preaching.

Valentine, remembering Fred Wilpon's vow that Jeff Wilpon would be seen but not heard for two years, later conveyed his disgust to the owner: "Have two years gone by already?" Valentine said to the elder Wilpon.

The following day, Valentine says he was told by Fred Wilpon that he had changed his mind: Valentine was fired.

"It happened so quickly," Valentine said in 2020. "It went from I was definitely coming back to I wasn't, and the only thing that happened in between was that [coaches'] meeting. I was coming back and then I wasn't."

Phillips, who remained as Mets general manager until June 2003, says he has no knowledge of the coaches' meeting Jeff Wilpon attended. It's Phillips' contention that a decision was reached to fire Valentine based on the team's performance and a desire for more harmony within the organization. Phillips says he had recommended to Fred Wilpon that Valentine be fired.

But Phillips was absent from the meeting in which Fred Wilpon fired Valentine.

"They didn't let me participate in it, I think just because at that point there was enough friction between Bobby and me, and they didn't want me to be in there with him," Phillips said. "Although I wish I had been able to be in there to at least be accountable for the decision. But I agreed with the decision that was made."

It was during that final meeting with Wilpon that Valentine, in disbelief he was fired, uttered the line, "I'm gone, but he gets to stay?"—a reference to Phillips.

If Valentine was in shock over the situation (aside from the fact he says Wilpon had previously told him his job was safe), it was because he thought he and Phillips would be evaluated as one unit. Wilpon had gone as far during a dinner with the manager and GM to tell them they were "attached at the hip" despite the rift that had grown between them.

The distrust between the manager and GM had started four years earlier, after Phillips was put on leave of absence by the club when a former Mets employee threatened to sue him for sexual harassment. Phillips, who was married, admitted to a consensual sexual relationship with the woman.

With Phillips suspended, Valentine made a comment at the general managers' meetings about the organization's need to move forward. That included not worrying about Phillips' opinion, because it was unknown if he would be returning. The comment got back to Phillips, who took it personally. Phillips returned to his job after a short absence, and Valentine began to resent the amount of access the GM had to Fred Wilpon.

Maybe no player was more affected by Valentine's firing than Alfonzo, who was set to become a free agent (he ultimately signed with the Giants) and entrusted Valentine with conveying a message to Fred Wilpon that he wanted to remain with the club.

"I was becoming a free agent, and the Mets were offering the same money that I signed for four years before," Alfonzo said. "And Bobby came to me and said, 'What are you looking for, because I am going to have a meeting with the Wilpons.' I liked being in New York, so if they gave me something reasonable I wanted to stay. Bobby said, 'Okay, I am going to talk to them, so you are looking for 20-something [million].'

"Then Bobby went and had a meeting with the Wilpons and I read in the paper that he got fired—the guy that was supposed to help me get a new contract. I was surprised, because I didn't think the Mets had it in mind to fire Bobby."

Valentine remains convinced it was his agitation about Jeff Wilpon's comments in the coaches' meeting that got him fired.

"It was all weird," Valentine said.

* * *

Phillips was charged with finding a new manager and compiled a list of candidates that included Buck Showalter and Terry Francona, while trying to extract Lou Piniella from his contract with the Mariners. The Mets were told they could have Piniella, but it would cost them a prospect. The Mariners wanted Double-A Binghamton shortstop Jose Reyes, who had stolen 58 bases the previous season.

The Mets chose another course. Art Howe had suddenly become available after guiding the Athletics to the postseason for a third straight year. Oakland general manager Billy Beane—whose organization was headed in a more analytically driven direction—had soured on his manager and asked Phillips if he might take Howe, who had one year remaining on his contract.

Phillips was smitten.

"The fact Art had won in Oakland was No. 1," said Jim Duquette, then the Mets assistant general manager. "And No. 2, when you met Art, he was one of the nicest human beings you have ever been around. He was the complete opposite of Bobby V. in the sense that people who knew Art said, 'If you want to have a good relationship with your manager you will be hard-pressed to have a better relationship than with Art. He is that nice of a man.'

"And when you are making that decision after jettisoning Bobby V., that became the prevailing factor rather than going full due diligence, seeing if Art could handle New York and obviously there were reasons Billy Beane was going to let him go: he didn't like the way he managed the team. But Steve kind of overlooked that because he was looking for a real good relationship with his next manager."

That charisma captivated Fred Wilpon, who said Howe "lit up the room" during their meeting. Howe received a four-year deal worth $9.4 million from the Mets—which nearly two decades later was still the biggest contract in franchise history for a manager.

Howe's personality was a contrast to the manner in which he was portrayed in *Moneyball*—the 2011 movie starring Brad Pitt based on Michael Lewis' book that detailed Oakland's use of statistical analysis to change the manner in which player performance was evaluated. Howe is portrayed by Phillip Seymour Hoffman in the movie and given the persona of a curmudgeon.

"People have a perception of Art Howe based on the movie *Moneyball* that is so slanted," Phillips said. "You could say whatever you want about Art, but nobody could say he's not a gentleman and a kind, good man. He didn't come across that way in the movie and I feel horrible for him for that.

"It's bizarre to me that is the way he was perceived, but I know he and Billy Beane did not get along all that well. I had a combative relationship sometimes with [Valentine] and Art had a combative relationship sometimes with Billy Beane, so I think he and I connected in a way where we thought we were getting a kinder, gentler relationship."

But as much as Howe charmed Wilpon and Phillips, he was overmatched by the New York media, which refused to accept "we battled" as the manager's default response to losses. Howe often wore a confused look when pressed on matters, and his handling of at least one sensitive situation may have eroded his credibility in the clubhouse.

As Piazza's skills at catcher deteriorated, team brass decided early in the 2003 season the future Hall of Famer should begin learning first base for a gradual transition. Howe, in a television interview, divulged the plan before it had been discussed with Piazza. The miscommunication left Piazza in the awkward position of receiving questions from reporters about a matter on which he hadn't been briefed. A soap opera had been hatched.

"I just think the New York market got to [Howe] to a degree," Phillips said. "Sometimes you look at guys and think, 'I don't know if that guy is really going to be able to handle New York.' Like I was really worried about John Olerud when we got him from Toronto. I was like, 'Boy, I don't know if he's going to be able to handle New York okay.' And then he lived in the city and took the No. 7 train to work every day, so you don't know, and Art I think was excited about the opportunity and felt like it was a good fit for him and New York was more aggressive than what he was ready for."

Cliff Floyd, who arrived as a free agent before Howe's first season with the Mets, compared the marriage between the team and manager to one he saw years later with his friend A.J. Burnett and the Yankees.

"Certain dudes are just meant for certain places," Floyd said. "A.J. Burnett called me before he went to the Yankees, and I was like, 'Nah, not New York.' He told me he was going. I said, 'Okay, I am just letting you know your personality is super dull, but people are going to look at you and want you to show emotion that you gave up five runs in the third inning.' And A.J. would be walking off the mound like those five runs are no big deal. I felt like [the fans] were going to destroy him there. It's not going to bother A.J., and he did okay in New York, but when he went to Pittsburgh you saw a different guy. I think certain players fit certain places and I felt like Art Howe didn't really fit to what Mets fans really thought their manager should be.

"No knock against Art Howe, it's just fans are really smart there and they wear their emotions on their sleeve. When Art was leaning on the top railing of the dugout, you should have heard the choice words they would give him every game. I didn't think it was right, but I just kept telling myself, 'We have names on the back of the jerseys and some of these names are Hall of Fame names, but we are getting them at the end of their careers.' Everybody was expecting that this team had to win 100 games, but I remember thinking, 'No, this ain't it.'"

* * *

Howe inherited the same flawed nucleus that got Valentine fired.

The GM had gambled that Vaughn, Alomar, Burnitz, and Cedeno still had significant productivity remaining, but was wrong on most counts. Vaughn, a Norwalk, Connecticut, native who starred at Seton Hall, had won an MVP award with the Red Sox before receiving a megadeal in free agency from the Angels. But Vaughn sustained a biceps injury that cost him the entire 2001 season and jeopardized his career.

Phillips had Kevin Appier's bad contract he wanted to unload, and after watching Vaughn work out just before Christmas in 2001 decided to take a shot.

"We had talked to the Angels and a lot of what I tried to manage was moving money for money," Phillips said. "I didn't want to add to the payroll, so how do I reconfigure our roster in a way by moving payroll to balance it out? I did a lot of that back then, where we trade Bernard Gilkey for Willie Blair and Jorge Fabregas and then flip Blair to Detroit and Fabregas to the Marlins to get out from beneath the Gilkey money. We were doing as much as we could toward flipping contracts so we could kind of free up finances."

After a respectable first season for the Mets in which he hit 26 homers, the overweight Vaughn had knee problems that prevented him from staying on the field. Vaughn played only 27 games for the Mets in 2003. The Mets had insurance on his contract, allowing them to recover a large percentage of the $34.3 million he received over the final two years of his deal.

Alomar was traded to the White Sox midway through 2003 after 1½ disappointing seasons with the Mets. Burnitz, another bust, was also traded before the end of the season.

"Burnitz gave you on-base percentage and power and Alomar was going to give us batting average, on-base percentage, steal a base, that prototypical switch-hitting guy that can turn the double play," Phillips said. "We thought it was a great deal for us and none of them played. They all underperformed in such a significant way and there was no exit strategy at the time. Where I had spun some contracts before there was no spinning to get out of these deals once they were in place and we sort of had to wait and let them play out a little bit."

One surprise addition was 37-year-old Tom Glavine, who had received minimal interest from the Braves after the 2002 season.

The left-hander wasn't a slam-dunk Hall of Famer at that point, but realized reaching 300 victories would provide a no-doubt ticket to Cooperstown. Glavine needed 58 wins to reach the plateau.

Greg Maddux and John Smoltz, who had joined Glavine in Atlanta to form the premier pitching rotation of the 1990s, were also on their way to the Hall of Fame. Glavine had finished 18–11 with a 2.96 ERA for the Braves in 2002, but it was the Mets and Phillies showing the strongest interest in his services as he reached free agency.

"Once it became apparent the Braves were less and less a reality for me it became more about trying to get somebody to give me that longer deal because I felt at that stage of the game [four years] was probably what I needed to get to 300 wins," Glavine said. "I didn't want to sign somewhere for three years and then have to go somewhere for a year to try to win 300 games. It was important to me if that fourth year wasn't guaranteed it was well within my reach through incentives or innings pitched."

Glavine agreed to a three-year deal with the Mets worth $35 million, with two vesting options that left the potential for a stay with the club through 2007. As it turned out, Glavine needed all five of those seasons to get his shot at his 300th victory.

The mission was accomplished on August 5, 2007, when Glavine beat the Cubs at Wrigley Field on a brutally humid night. Glavine had whiffed in his first attempt at the milestone in his previous start, in Milwaukee.

"I remember really wanting to get it over with because my teammates were getting hounded about it and I didn't like that and I wanted to get it over for them—maybe not as much as I wanted it for myself, obviously—but I wanted to get it over for them," Glavine said. "The venue of Wrigley Field and my parents being there, my dad being a huge baseball fan and never having been to Wrigley Field, and for him to be there and see that ballpark, see it all happen, it was a surreal night."

Two years later, Randy Johnson won his 300th game—wearing a Giants uniform in a final season—and no pitcher has approached the milestone since. Given the manner baseball has changed in recent years, with wins becoming more difficult to accumulate for a starting pitcher, it's possible the game will never again see a 300-game winner.

Put in that context, Glavine is even more appreciative of reaching the plateau.

"Randy did it after me and was the last guy and most likely will be the last guy," Glavine said. "When you think about it in those terms, to be one of the last guys to ever do something, and then be part of such a small group of guys in the history of the game that did something, it's a big deal.

"I don't think the way the game is today, more than anything else with how hard these guys are throwing and the effort they use night in and night out on every pitch, you have to pitch 20 years to do it and I just don't see anybody staying healthy for 20 years anymore."

* * *

The losses were tough enough for Steve Phillips to accept in 2003, but then came the death threats.

At the time, Phillips says he was resigned to the fact he would soon be fired, after Wilpon had spared him the previous offseason when Valentine was axed.

Art Howe "lit up the room" in his managerial interview with owner Fred Wilpon. But in his two seasons as Mets manager, Howe appeared overmatched by his environment.

"I remember going into Fred's booth one day during a weekend day game and I remember watching the game and I just said, 'Fred, so you understand, I know how this all works.'"

In early May, the Mets were 11–17 when Mike Vaccaro wrote a particularly scathing column in the *New York Post* that used graphic imagery. Phillips referenced that column in 2019 when discussing the final days of his Mets tenure.

"But few teams in history have ever been this hated, this reviled, this scorned, this loathed by their own fans," Vaccaro wrote. "Fans of bad teams tend to be apathetic, or sad, or angry, or disillusioned. I spent a year in Kansas City, watching a wretched Royal team commit baseball felonies every day. People booed. People wanted the manager fired, the GM fired, the players traded, the usual soundtrack of a lost summer.

"But Mets fans want people *dead.*"

Vaccaro continued: "They don't want Steve Phillips fired as much as they want his head fixed to a pike, displayed on the Triborough Bridge as a warning to future incompetents. They don't want to just run Mo Vaughn and Robbie Alomar and Roger Cedeno out of town, they want them driven through the streets, wrapped in their contracts, big targets on their backs so they can have rocks thrown at them before they get to the city limits."

Phillips confronted Vaccaro the following day in the visitor's clubhouse in Milwaukee. The conversation got heated and personal, to the point Mets director of media relations Jay Horwitz interceded to ensure it wouldn't turn into a physical altercation.

Already, Phillips had been receiving death threats—one of which prevented him from going on the field during batting practice on a trip to Montreal with the club. Later, he would also be told by MLB security to avoid going on the field during batting practice in Philadelphia.

"I had threats, stalkers, I had to have security getting me from the team bus into the hotel and from the hotel into the stadium," Phillips said.

Security officials eventually found the person making the threats.

"Literally, they followed the guy and came back and said, 'Look, we're not sure he would hurt you, but he might kill himself in front of you,'" Phillips said. "I had another guy who showed up and I ended up getting a restraining order because he figured if I was giving money to players he wanted money, and he came around a few times."

Wilpon fired Phillips on June 12, 2003, with the Mets sitting at 29–35. Phillips' replacement was Duquette, who had spent 11 years in the organization working his way to assistant GM. For Phillips, it was almost a relief to be fired.

Though he says he later received feelers to work in front office jobs for other teams, Phillips says he was spent. He took an analyst position with ESPN—he was fired from the network in 2009 after it was revealed he was having an affair with a production assistant—and later began hosting a show on SiriusXM's MLB Network radio.

"I had zero desire to pursue [front-office work]," Phillips said. "The job is a lifestyle, it's not a job. It's 162 games and then the work starts and I am one that can get consumed by the intensity and the anxiety, the stress and pressure of it all and I know at the end of my tenure it ate me up. It really had eaten me up—physically, mentally, emotionally, spiritually—and it wasn't anything I had any desire to get back in, which is kind of why I went into the media side of it.

"At the end of the day somebody wins, somebody loses, and I don't get a call from an owner or an owner's son or the media and I don't have to feel good or bad because the team is winning or losing. The competitive part of it was I just had to keep working to be the best at whatever I was doing, because we all have that competitive sort of gene we need to satisfy. But I didn't have any real desire to get back in to be a GM again."

Valentine and Phillips have since mended their relationship, appearing together on the banquet circuit and at charity golf outings. Valentine, after returning to Japan as a manager and winning a championship, had a turbulent season managing the Red Sox in 2012 (he was fired following a player mutiny) before becoming the athletic director at Sacred Heart University in Fairfield, Connecticut. In 2019, Phillips' son was a standout high school football player in Connecticut who was recruited by Sacred Heart. According to Valentine, it's fair to term his relationship with Phillips as cordial.

"I have reached out to Steve a bunch of times," Valentine said. "It was tough for him for a while, but I had him up at school. I have gotten him speaking engagements where he has gone out and made a couple of bucks. I have been on his show any time he wants to call."

Phillips blames himself for much of the friction that occurred between Valentine and himself.

"I was immature at times," Phillips said. "I was so young getting that job and I didn't speak up in a way, say things in a way that I should have. I look back at it as a fond relationship and I remember Bobby the great instructor and coach. I remember the hugs when we won playoff games and qualifying for the playoffs and wild card and going to the World Series and remember those far more than I remember any of the disagreements."

* * *

Rick Peterson was going through a rough divorce and needed a job that would place him back on the East Coast, close to his three sons in New Jersey.

It was just before the 2003 season, and Peterson had signed a new four-year contract to remain as Oakland's pitching coach, after helping develop Tim Hudson, Barry Zito, and Mark Mulder into as formidable a 1-2-3 rotation punch as the American League had seen in recent years. Peterson's plan was to relocate his family from New Jersey to the Oakland area with the security of this new contract, but that all changed when his wife filed for divorce.

Suddenly, Peterson was separated from his three sons and regretted signing the new contract. As the first season concluded he begged Billy Beane to let him escape the deal. Beane at first resisted—Peterson, an early disciple of analytics, was regarded among the game's best pitching coaches—but ultimately the GM's humanity prevailed. Beane volunteered to call the Mets, who already had Peterson's former dugout accomplice Howe and were looking for a new direction with the pitching staff.

Peterson first interviewed with Duquette, who told him he had the job as long as Fred Wilpon and Jeff Wilpon approved of the hiring. Peterson recalled that during his subsequent meeting with the owners, Fred Wilpon asked why he wanted to leave Oakland, which had reached the playoffs in four straight years with an elite pitching staff, to join the Mets.

"I said, 'Fred, there are only three reasons: Sean, Derek, and Dylan,'" Peterson said, referring to his three sons.

Peterson got the job. As compensation to Oakland, the Mets surrendered a pick in the Rule 5 draft.

Peterson's staff with the Mets featured a pair of 38-year-olds in Tom Glavine and Al Leiter, with Steve Trachsel, Kris Benson, and Jae Weong Seo filling out the rotation. It was hardly the group Peterson had overseen in Oakland.

With the Mets sputtering at midseason, team brass looked to inject a high-upside arm into the rotation and viewed Tampa Bay's Victor Zambrano as a strong possibility. The cost would be the organization's top pitching prospect, Scott Kazmir.

A 20-year-old left-hander, Kazmir had been selected by the Mets in the first round of the previous year's draft, but there were concerns about an irregularity in his elbow—a condition that had led team officials to question whether they should offer him a full signing bonus.

Before his first full season in the minors began, Kazmir flew to Birmingham, Alabama, with Peterson and other team officials on Jeff Wilpon's private jet to receive a biomechanical analysis. Aaron Heilman was also part of the traveling party and received an analysis.

"We looked at the biomechanical analysis and made some adjustments in [Kazmir's] delivery that spring and then he went to the minor leagues," Peterson said.

Months later, the pitching coach was told the Mets were entertaining the idea of trading Kazmir for Zambrano. Peterson was asked for his opinion, but said he didn't know Zambrano, other than from watching him pitch against Oakland.

Peterson received an invitation to Howe's office, where Duquette and Jeff Wilpon were also present. The group watched video of Zambrano, and Peterson was asked for his opinion. Peterson provided a breakdown of the right-hander's delivery as the others listened.

At one point Duquette was used as a prop as Peterson attempted to explain a glitch in Zambrano's delivery that perhaps explained why a pitcher with electric stuff had never reached his full potential. The fix was simple in Peterson's estimation, but only if Zambrano was committed to practicing the change in delivery. Zambrano's athleticism—he had played shortstop in the minor leagues—left Peterson optimistic he was amenable to the change.

As the trade deadline approached, top team officials and scouts conversed on a conference call with Peterson, as the Mets prepared to play in Montreal. The group exchanged opinions on Zambrano and whether he was worth Tampa Bay's asking price of Kazmir. Toward the end of the call, which included more than a dozen voices, Peterson was asked by Duquette about Zambrano's delivery, as previously studied on video.

Peterson explained that Zambrano's delivery needed adjustments.

"But we'll take him down to the bullpen and we'll make a couple of adjustments and then you have got to practice it," Peterson says he told the group. "It takes about 10 minutes and then you do some drills and start practicing it and then he should get it pretty quickly."

The Mets opted for the deal, sending Kazmir and Jose Diaz to Tampa Bay for the 29-year-old Zambrano and Bartolome Fortunato. And Peterson's legacy with the Mets was about to be formed, based on a message that emanated through the airwaves following the trade.

"My oldest son called me and said, 'Dad, I just finished watching *Baseball Tonight* on ESPN and Tim Kurkjian said you can fix Zambrano in 10 minutes,'" Peterson said.

Irate, Peterson called the reporter and demanded an explanation.

"I would never say that about Zambrano, number one—my mind doesn't even think that way," Peterson said. "I don't think about fixing people. I think about untapping potential."

Peterson was informed that a team official on the conference call had leaked the idea that the pitching coach could perform a quick fix on Zambrano. But to Peterson, nothing good could come from the public receiving such a notion. His fear was hearing on WFAN that "Rick Peterson thinks he can fix Zambrano in 10 minutes."

It was too late. The legend that Peterson could fix Zambrano in 10 minutes had been born and there wouldn't be any turning back.

Zambrano was dealing with elbow discomfort, a fact unbeknownst to the Mets until after the trade was complete. Less than three weeks after arriving in the deal, Zambrano walked off the mound in Colorado in pain and wouldn't return for the remainder of the season.

Duquette and team medical personnel rechecked the paperwork to see if something had been missed before the trade. Nothing was discovered. It's the Mets' contention that Tampa Bay withheld information before the deal, but as Duquette and Peterson sought a nullification of the trade, Jeff Wilpon told them the matter wouldn't be pursued. The fact Zambrano had already started three games for the Mets weakened their position in a potential fight with Tampa Bay. After the season the Mets overhauled their medical staff, clearly displeased that something had been missed with Zambrano.

"At that point when Zambrano was injured there was a lot of finger-pointing going on and a lot of backbiting," Duquette said. "The doctors were the ones who missed it. They [the team doctors] also thought Kazmir would get injured because he had an elbow issue. When we signed [Kazmir] there was some consternation over whether we should sign him because there was an irregularity in the elbow. It was enough of a concern that we questioned whether we should offer him a full signing bonus or not. We had that kind of in the back of our minds: there is a bone spur that is eventually going to turn to bone chip, which also means the ligament is compromised and he's going to end up having Tommy John surgery."

The Mets received a full 2005 season from Zambrano, but the following year he tore the flexor tendon in his elbow after only five starts, essentially ending his career—he pitched briefly for the Orioles and Blue Jays in a comeback attempt.

"The last pitch he threw [with the Mets] he ran off the mound, and I followed him after the inning was over," Peterson said. "They were doing some kind of X-ray and he had his head on my chest crying like a five-year-old. And he said, 'Rick, if only I could have pitched one day healthy for this team.' He had a pain tolerance like you can't believe."

Kazmir spent 12 years in the major leagues and compiled a 108–96 record with a 4.01 ERA. The fact he had been a ballyhooed first-round pick and Zambrano was such a bust put the trade on a short list among the worst in franchise history. The worst is generally regarded as the deal that sent Nolan Ryan to the Angels for Jim Fregosi following the 1971 season.

Adam Fisher, who worked 14 years in the Mets front office, said Peterson shouldn't be completely exonerated in the failed Kazmir trade. But Fisher puts the blame on the organization as a whole.

"[Peterson] at that time was sort of at peak power and puffing his chest out a little bit and that definitely was a factor," Fisher said. "I don't think it was the only factor. At the end of the day it comes down to who you got back, not that you traded Kazmir, but that you got Victor Zambrano back and it was a very lopsided trade right from the start. You don't trade a top-20 prospect for a player who needs to be fixed. You can't fix that type of command. It was never a good idea."

In a strange twist, Kazmir and Peterson were reunited years after the deal. At the time Kazmir was rebounding from injury and attempting to revive his career. Peterson, who had been fired by the Mets a year earlier, received a call from Kazmir's agent asking him to work with the left-hander. Peterson agreed to work with Kazmir, but not until Rays officials, most notably manager Joe Maddon and general manager Jim Hickey, gave their blessings.

"Sure enough, I talk to Joe Maddon and Jim Hickey, and Scott Kazmir comes down to the Jersey Shore and I get his biomechanical analysis and we go through this whole process and we're on this high school field," Peterson said.

The following day Peterson asked Kazmir to work out with him in Manhattan, where the former pitching coach planned to visit his girlfriend, who later became his second wife. The drills wouldn't involve any throwing. Peterson was set to meet Kazmir at a small park before a friend reminded him how the whole scene could be perceived in New York City.

"People are going to walk by going, 'You couldn't fix Zambrano in 10 minutes, now you are fixing Kazmir?'" Peterson said, laughing about his friend's warning. "I was like, what the hell, I didn't even think of that. Can you imagine that story, right?"

The two ultimately found a yoga studio for their workout, and the next day Kazmir threw a bullpen session also out of sight. Peterson says he received a call from Tampa Bay's Andrew Freidman about a week later informing him that Kazmir's velocity had jumped and he was throwing the best change-up team officials had seen from him.

Peterson was still with the Mets years earlier when he ventured into a grocery store in New York one offseason for a can of crushed tomatoes.

"I go out and I have got this old leather jacket on and a baseball-type cap on and I got the can of tomatoes and this lady is behind me and she's like in her mid-seventies, her hair looked like Einstein, and she is leaning over the cart, she was short and obviously couldn't hear very well so she talked loud, and told me she knew who I was," Peterson said.

The woman told Peterson she was a huge Mets fan and had one question for him.

"Is the 10 minutes up on Zambrano yet?" the woman asked him.

"And then there were two other lines and they were going, 'Yeah, Rick, what's going on with Zambrano? Is the 10 minutes up?'"

Peterson's legacy with the Mets is his failure to fix Zambrano, but the pitching coach was instrumental in helping Glavine pitch respectably into his forties, just as the strike zone was changing. At the time MLB had instituted QuesTech—a virtual replay system that forced umpires to change the strike zone to the rule book definition.

For the previous decade-plus, Glavine had lived on the outside corner, receiving strike calls on pitches that were just off the plate.

"I have to give [Peterson] a ton of credit for saving or resurrecting the last three years of my career," Glavine said. "The strike zone changed from being the east-west strike zone that I had pitched to for so many years and now it was north-south. I was stubborn—adamant that I was not going to change.

"Rick was the one instrumental in talking me off the ledge a little bit and making me realize that, 'Okay, things are different now and here's how you are going to combat it.'"

Glavine recalled listening in disbelief as Peterson preached pitching inside 50 percent of the time. Glavine says he was probably only throwing inside six to eight pitches a game to right-handed hitters at that point in his career.

"I thought Rick was nuts," Glavine said. "I finally came around to his way of thinking and I started doing it and I started having success.

"At the stage of my game my favorite analogy that he used with me, he said, 'Look, Tiger Woods is the greatest golfer in the game and he goes out there and plays with 14 clubs in his bag.' He doesn't go out there and play with two clubs. Let's play with the 14 clubs in your bag and that was all an effort to use both sides of the plate…and not pigeonhole myself not being what I was for so many years."

* * *

As a dismal 2004 season neared conclusion, the Mets were headed toward another regime change. Despite the fact he had two years and $4.7 million left on his contract, the overmatched Howe was informed in mid-September that he was fired. In an odd twist, Howe agreed to stay on as manager for the final 2½ weeks of the season. Duquette was later fired, replaced by Omar Minaya, who was returning to the organization after overseeing the Expos during a three-year stretch in which the team was run by MLB.

The 38-year-old Leiter had pitched at a respectable level for the Mets, finishing 10–8 with a 3.21 ERA in 30 starts and had a strong desire to end his career with the team. Leiter reached a verbal agreement with Duquette on a one-year deal to return, but when the GM was fired those plans changed.

"Omar came in and was like, 'Hang tight, we will circle back to this,'" Leiter said. "It had all the makings of them wanting to do the right thing by me, but they didn't really want me back and it was very obvious at least through my communication with my agents."

Leiter received offers from the Marlins and Yankees, opting for a return to South Florida, where he still owned a home. But after seven seasons of playing for the team he loved growing up, leaving the Mets was difficult. Left unfilled was his goal of reaching 100 wins with the team, which would have placed him fourth in franchise history behind the iconic trio of Tom Seaver, Dwight Gooden, and Jerry Koosman. Leiter finished his Mets career at 95–67, sixth in wins (Ron Darling and Sid Fernandez were also ahead of him).

"My desire to stay with the Mets was huge," Leiter said. "I wanted five more wins to get 100 as a Met and be fourth all-time in the history of the franchise. It mattered to me to be behind brand names in Tom Seaver, Jerry Koosman, and Dwight Gooden. I needed five more wins to be fourth and I really wanted that and I was maybe a baby bitch for a while after I didn't get the opportunity to sign back with the Mets, but it's all good. Life takes you in different ways."

Minaya had bigger plans and signed Pedro Martinez to a four-year contract worth $54 million, giving the Mets two future Hall of Famers on the back end of their careers in the same rotation (Glavine was the other). At 33 years old, Martinez was no longer the overwhelming force who had electrified Fenway Park for most of his seven seasons in Boston, but his value remained high after helping the Red Sox win the World Series the previous year, ending an 86-year drought for the franchise. Martinez, who had battled shoulder problems, was coming off a season in which he finished 16–9 with a career-worst 3.90 ERA.

Martinez was largely detested by the other fan base in New York, with a brawl between the Yankees and Red Sox during Game 3 of the ALCS in 2003 serving as the punctuation mark. During the chaos, Martinez shoved Don Zimmer to the ground, sending the 72-year-old Yankees bench coach to the hospital.

By signing Martinez, the Mets saw an opportunity to reclaim back page headlines that had eluded them in recent seasons. Martinez rebounded in 2005 and finished 15–8 with a 2.82 ERA in 31 starts for a team that remained interesting for most of the season.

"Pedro was the poster child of being able to reinvent yourself in the game," Cliff Floyd said. "Everybody thinks reinventing yourself is a bad thing. No, it's when you try to reinvent the wheel. Reinventing the wheel is when you have good stuff, but your ass tries to do something totally different than you are capable of doing. Reinventing yourself to me is what Pedro started. Pedro was like, 'I don't throw 98 mph anymore, I have got to rely on my change-up and my curveball has got to get better. My fastball has got to be placed 90–92 in the right spot,' and that is what he was able to do and that is why we respected him. Some guys just want to take the money and come to New York and just go away peacefully. He wasn't about that life."

* * *

It became obvious as the 2005 season concluded that Piazza, who had turned 37 in September, wouldn't be re-signed by the Mets. Banged up, Piazza appeared in only 113 games that season and hit 19 homers. Two years earlier, he had played only 68 games for the Mets because of a torn groin.

The Mets had tried converting Piazza into a part-time first baseman, but the transition was a difficult one. Piazza started 66 games at first base in 2004, before the experiment was abandoned the following season.

Piazza, years later, admitted he probably should have taken seriously the idea of playing first base earlier in his career. But such a switch also would have impacted his chances of finishing as the all-time home run leader as a catcher. Piazza hit homer No. 352 as a catcher on May 5, 2004, breaking the record set by Carlton Fisk.

"Maybe it was a mistake, in the later years in the '90s maybe I could have taken some ground balls at first base," Piazza said. "Maybe from a selfish standpoint I just wanted to beat the home run record for catchers, and from a selfish standpoint I could have gotten a few more years and gotten more money. Maybe if I was playing some decent first base into my later years I could have caught a little bit, played some first base and go to the American League and DH.

"I did try to become an adequate first baseman, but then I realized at that point I was in 'old dog, new tricks,' territory. And I don't think I had the age and the vigor to become a good first baseman or an adequate fielding major league first baseman at that point.... It was tough, because my contract was backloaded, so they were paying me a lot of money the last two years. And the team was like, 'We are paying this guy millions of dollars and we can't make him a part-time catcher and he's got to play every day.'"

Piazza signed with the Padres and had a resurgence, before joining the Athletics to finish his career in 2007.

"Eight years in New York for a player is a pressure cooker," Piazza said. "They hired Willie [Randolph] and I remember the last year Willie was hitting me fifth, then sixth and then seventh, and the media was coming to me asking me if it was an insult. I'm like, 'If he hits me ninth, I'm going to fucking go out there and hit ninth and do the best I can.'"

* * *

Gary Cohen faced a major career decision following the 2005 season. After 17 seasons in the Mets radio booth, where he ascended to lead announcer following Bob Murphy's retirement, Cohen emerged as a candidate to become SNY's first play-by-play voice. The team-owned network was set to debut in 2006, bringing a shake-up to an existing TV booth that included Dave O'Brien, Ted Robinson, Fran Healy, Tom Seaver, and Keith Hernandez.

The play-by-play position was offered to O'Brien, but he declined after receiving a new contract from ESPN—where he had been calling games in addition to his part-time Mets duties. O'Brien called Cohen and told him he should pursue the SNY job.

"I had no interest," Cohen said. "I had never been a TV guy. I'm still not a TV guy."

Cohen had been embraced by Mets fans since his arrival to the radio booth in 1989. Meticulous in his preparation and polished in delivery,

Cohen was considered the perfect complement to Murphy, the familiar voice who had joined Lindsey Nelson and Ralph Kiner in the 1960s and '70s to give the Mets their first iconic broadcast team. Later, Tim McCarver joined Kiner to give the Mets another legendary broadcast team, on television. Murphy switched strictly to radio for the duration of his career.

"Murph had his own way of doing things," Cohen said. "He was a very by-the-book announcer and there wasn't a lot of levity or a lot of sidetracking."

Cohen's first season in the booth included 23 spring training games with Murphy, as WFAN looked to fill air time in the afternoon. By the end of the year, Mike Francesa had been paired with Chris Russo, giving the station a dynamic talk-show combo that lasted for nearly two decades.

"They didn't have a strong afternoon lineup [in 1989] so they wanted to do as many spring training games as possible," Cohen said. "It actually worked out great for me because it gave me a lot of practice with Murph during spring training. He was light and happy and we would shoot the shit during games back and forth and it was all fun and games.

"And then Opening Day came and I was completely unprepared for this because I figured it would stay the way it was. But the blinders went on and [Murphy] did the straight-ahead broadcast and I had to adjust to that. It was a learning experience for me, but Murph knew exactly what he wanted to do and knew exactly what he wanted me to do, so we figured it out. We worked 15 years together and it evolved over time."

Murphy retired following the 2003 season, opening a seat for Howie Rose, who had previously served as the Mets' lead TV voice. The versatile Rose was also the voice of the New York Islanders on television following a stint in the New York Rangers radio booth. Rose had been covering the Mets since the 1980s as a host and reporter for WFAN. Cohen and Rose were both New Yorkers and brought a certain chemistry to the booth.

"After Murph retired we had our two years together in '04 and '05, which for me were just off the charts, the most fun I've ever had doing radio or TV," Cohen said. "It was like working with a brother from another mother. Howie and I, we grew up in different places from within Queens, but so much of our experience was similar and yet we look at things sometimes differently. At every point we were able to find common ground and find different ways of talking about the same thing. It was a spectacularly fun experience."

The SNY job was more prestigious, but Cohen had a difficult time fathoming a departure from the radio booth. Chief among his concerns was he would be precluded from calling Mets postseason games. Those productions were handled by the national networks and cable outlets.

Cohen ultimately accepted SNY's offer, putting him in the same booth with Hernandez, who was told early on he would be retained for the new network. SNY brass wanted a second analyst, preferably a pitcher, and offered the job to Al Leiter, but he wasn't comfortable with the idea of a full-time workload. David Cone was another candidate for the position, but he also wasn't prepared to commit to a full schedule.

Ron Darling had become aware of the new network months earlier, when Hernandez mentioned it to him before a game in Washington, telling him he should apply for a position. At the time, Darling was in his first year working TV broadcasts for the Nationals. He had been offered the Nationals job only three days before the season started. The catch was Darling had to work the full schedule.

"All in, 162 games, see if not only I have the stamina for it, but the love for it," Darling said, recalling his rationale in accepting the Nationals TV job. "I wasn't very good and I was learning on the job and was very green, but I did learn I have the stamina for it. I did learn I have the love for it, and those two things probably put me in the right place when SNY came calling."

Darling auditioned with the network's executives and listened as they provided him with suggestions that might improve his work. The fact he was willing to work a full schedule ultimately gave him the job.

Hernandez was friendly with Darling at the time—they had been teammates for most of the 1980s and shared a World Series title together—but the two hardly had what could be described as a tight relationship.

"Ronnie was aloof when he played—very aloof—which is fine," Hernandez said. "We got along fine. We did hang out on occasion, but Ronnie was more of a loner, so our relationship really has grown, our friendship."

Darling says a generational divide between him and Hernandez (who is seven years older than him) was part of the reason maybe they weren't tight as teammates.

"Keith and I went to dinner and we dated girls that were really best friends, so to say we didn't see each other would be wrong," Darling said. "We saw each other a lot, but I wouldn't say we had a lot in common. Keith is much more social than I and he was a fully formed individual when we were playing and confident and I was none of those. He is a different generation, so I honestly paid more homage and respect to him than I did being a friend to him."

Both former Mets were also learning to mesh with Cohen, whom they had known during their playing days, but only in passing. Darling says a sense of "vulnerability" bonded the trio in SNY's first season.

"Gary was coming from radio, I was coming from nothing and Keith was going to do a full schedule for the first time...so we really worked hard," Darling said. "Gary to me is probably as good as anyone doing games on television. He was probably the best in the world on the radio side, but nobody really carried any ego into it."

The tension-breaker, as Darling recalls, came only moments before the trio's first broadcast together. At the time, Darling was concerned that he and Hernandez might step on each other on the air.

"It was a minute or two before we went on the air for the first time and Keith in his succinct, brilliant way said, 'Remember, you do the pitching and I do the hitting,'" Darling said. "Honestly, in that one sentence he took care of all the things that three-man booths lack, and that's the traffic is always difficult. Keith took care of it one sentence right before we went on the air."

Darling has become the most visible of the group, with his national presence on TBS' postseason coverage each October. But Hernandez's popularity perhaps remains the highest given his off-the-cuff style and fame from his appearances in the sitcom *Seinfeld* in the 1990s. In later years, Hernandez has become a presence on Twitter, where he offers musings about his cat, Hadji.

I asked Hernandez if he believes his popularity is higher post-playing days than it was when he starred for the Mets.

"People saw me play and saw this intense, in on every play, going to the mound, playing with emotion and they thought I was just this Genghis Khan or something," Hernandez said. "Going into the booth allowed me to be who I am. I'm sarcastic. I have an acerbic sense of humor. I am off-the-cuff. I think people were stunned that I was this other person, which is the real me.

"Am I more popular now? I do reach more people, different generations. If I had quit and said goodbye the younger generation never would have known me.... Now I reach other generations because I am in the booth, so I guess I am more popular and that makes me very happy."

Darling was diagnosed with thyroid cancer in 2019 and underwent surgery that kept him removed from the booth for much of the season. A scare occurred after the surgery, as Darling could not speak; his vocal cords had been bruised.

For two months he underwent extensive rehab, receiving steroids and injections that allowed his voice to regain the strength needed for a return to the job. He estimates his voice is only 60 percent of where it was previously, but says it's "passable" for the broadcast booth. But the experience has left Darling to wonder how much longer he might continue in the job.

"I would hope that if we could, it would be nice that Gary and I and Keith somehow make a run, whatever those years will be, and we all go out at the same time," Darling said. "I think that would be a good way to do it. I don't know if we'll be able to do it, but I am hoping that happens."

Hernandez, who at 66 years old received a three-year contract from SNY that runs through 2022, has visions of working into his seventies.

"I don't want to be 80 years old and doing this, but I kind of would like to gradually phase out and do fewer and fewer games and never really give it up," Hernandez said. "But I don't want to be in that booth too long, where I am not effective."

A colleague has suggested Cohen might want to end his career in the Mets radio booth, allowing him to come full circle. It's an idea Cohen won't completely dismiss.

"I love radio," Cohen said. "I love the people I work with at SNY and if I wasn't working with such incredible people—and I don't only mean Ronnie and Keith—then that would be different. You never know what is going to happen down the road, but I do love radio. It's definitely what I was meant to do. I still think in radio and speak in TV. It's almost like two different languages."

CHAPTER 3
BUT NOT
GOOD ENOUGH

Billy Wagner will now admit it: he authored the infamous note. The target was Lastings Milledge, a free-spirited rookie who had ignored the time-honored tradition of newcomers keeping a low profile and earning their place in the game. Milledge arrived on the scene in 2006 as the youngest player in the National League at 21 years old, after emerging as the Mets' next great prospect.

Milledge could hit for power and average, run, and throw. He also had a flamboyant side that was on display in June when he homered in the 10th inning against Armando Benitez—then pitching for the Giants—to tie the game at Shea Stadium. Upon returning to the field, Milledge high-fived the fans seated in the front row for his entire route to right field.

It was just the latest Milledge transgression that had alienated the veterans in a season the Mets would win their first NL East title since 1988. Milledge had a tendency to speak when others believed he should be listening and to follow his own rules.

As the Mets regular season prepared to conclude, at decrepit RFK Stadium in Washington, a note appeared above Milledge's locker: "KNOW YOUR PLACE, ROOK!"—signed, YOUR TEAMMATES.

Wagner was identified in media reports as the note's author, but has never spoken publicly in great detail about the matter until now.

"I put the note in there because [Milledge] had a tendency to say things and at that point you have got to know where you stand," Wagner said. "That locker room is sacred, and you do things, there's just things that you don't do and there's things that you can do. The rookies, there's not a lot you can be doing and saying and complaining about. You are in the big leagues and you are getting a lot of things done for you. You are there to contribute and you are the 25th man most of the time, you are not that No. 1 guy. You are not David Wright. You are not Tom Glavine. So you have got to know your spot and your role and when you can't do that, that is when the older guys kind of say, 'Hey, you need to know your role.'"

Wagner, an All-Star reliever who arrived to the Mets before the 2006 season, was known almost as much for his gigantic clubhouse presence as his huge fastball. In an era when 96 mph was still elite heat, Wagner and his gifted left arm stood apart in the game.

The clubhouse included veterans such as Glavine, Cliff Floyd, Carlos Delgado, and Carlos Beltran, but the role of enforcer fell upon the straight-shooter Wagner, who had received his own schooling as a young player with the Astros. It was during those years he had seen rookie players fall into disfavor with teammates for something as trivial as refusing to carry the beer bag to the bus.

"There were many times I was told to shut up, stay in my space, and you have to learn those things," Wagner said. "There's been a lot of things said about me doing that to Milledge, but these guys that wouldn't say things to him needed to say things to him. The locker rooms I was in [with Houston], there probably wouldn't have been a sign. Ken Caminiti would not have put a sign on my locker telling me to stay in my place. He would have been in your face and you know those things.

"Politely, [the sign] was the best thing that could happen, because David Wright is not going to say anything to Milledge. I am sure Cliff did, but Milledge just wouldn't listen. It was really a team thing that needed to be just that. It didn't need to be any more than…just keep your mouth shut and know where you're supposed to be and stay in your lane."

Omar Minaya, who had been hired as Mets general manager before the previous season, remembered Beltran giving advice to Milledge at various points. Arriving to the ballpark on the later bus was a no-no for rookies, but Milledge was a repeat offender who needed lecturing.

"The players tried," Minaya said. "Beltran and others started talking to him and tried to give him advice. But major league players in this generation, they will give you advice, but they are not going to overdo it. They tell you once and that's it. [Milledge] was a good kid, but people once they tell you something, they want to see some follow-up. Lastings at the time had a lot of other things besides baseball on his mind. Like a lot of young kids, the focus wasn't there at the time."

Floyd recalled spending a bus ride to Philadelphia, at the behest of manager Willie Randolph, trying to get Milledge to change his attitude. Floyd entered the conversation realizing he was probably wasting his time, but says he tried for the team's sake.

The conversation concluded with Floyd telling Milledge to arrive earlier than normal at the ballpark for an upcoming 1:00 PM game so they could put in extra work in the batting cage, showing the veterans the rookie took his job seriously.

"That is when all hell broke loose," Floyd said.

Floyd arrived early at Citizens Bank Park on the agreed day and waited for Milledge. Floyd finally gave up. About an hour before first pitch, long past the required reporting time, Milledge entered the clubhouse casually, wearing his backpack, and in front of teammates began checking the lineup card to see if he was playing.

"You would think he would try to slide in, take his backpack off, and maybe call me and say, 'I messed up again, can you slide me some shorts and a T-shirt out in the hallway and I can go change real quick and act like I have been here,'" Floyd said. "He walks in and proceeds to check the lineup to see if he's playing. Obviously, Willow took him out of the lineup. I'm just over there and trying to keep my composure.... Milledge had a lot of those moments. He just had too many moments when he couldn't get out of his own way.

"It's just one of those things, prospects turn to suspects but usually they are the culprit. It's not a case of where you were in a bad system and you got evaluated the wrong way. No, you get more chances than anybody. It was just unfortunate, because I thought he had a good shot."

Milledge was largely a disappointment in his two seasons with the team. He was traded to the Nationals following the 2007 season in a deal that brought Ryan Church and Brian Schneider to the Mets. Later,

Milledge bounced to the Pirates and White Sox, playing his last major league game in 2011.

Wright says the Mets—and Wagner in particular—didn't cross the line with their treatment of Milledge.

"As a younger player I enjoyed when the veteran guys got on me, because it felt like I was part of a unit, part of a team," Wright said. "It was almost like the elementary school, playground mentality. Lastings went right back at [Wagner], so it wasn't like this was one-sided. Lastings would make fun of his cowboy boots, so it was two-sided and back-and-forth and I think oftentimes you say one of the players was attacked or something, but my experience with the whole situation, most of the time it's playful banter and the guys know how to take it."

Wagner, who has become a successful high school baseball coach in Charlottesville, Virginia, said he was criticized by Randolph for the manner in which he treated Milledge. It was one of several clashes between the closer and manager during their 2½ seasons together.

"Willie got on me about giving [Milledge] a hard time," Wagner said. "It was one of those things that really got overblown because Milledge was young."

* * *

Rick Peterson's entire baseball life flashed before his eyes as Beltran fell behind 0–2 in the count in Game 7 of the 2006 NLCS. It was the ninth inning of a classic game against the Cardinals, with the Mets' season hinging on whether Beltran could deliver against Adam Wainwright with two outs and the bases loaded.

In the 20 seconds or so before Wainwright would deliver his next pitch, Peterson, the Mets pitching coach, began reflecting on his journey to reach this point, over a lifetime. The son of a Pirates executive—Harding "Pete" Peterson was also briefly the Yankees' general manager in

1990—Rick Peterson had grown up around Roberto Clemente and Willie Stargell and reveled in Pittsburgh's World Series titles in 1960, '71, and '79. As a major league coach, Peterson had never been to the World Series.

"To relive all that in 20 seconds…and my last thought, I was coming back to the present as a pitching coach and my last thought was, 'Wainwright is throwing a breaking ball right here,'" Peterson said.

Beltran had tied Todd Hundley's franchise record by hitting 41 homers during the regular season. He had hit three more in this NLCS, giving him 11 homers in 18 career postseason games. The Mets' season now hinged on their best player delivering with the bases loaded.

Already, there had been plenty of drama, from Endy Chavez's full mid-air suspension catch reaching over Shea Stadium's left-field fence to rob Scott Rolen of a two-run homer in the sixth to Oliver Perez's heroic six innings on short rest in which he allowed only one run.

The Cardinals had somehow snuck into the playoffs with only 83 wins, but possessed a stud in Albert Pujols in the middle of their lineup, surrounding him with Rolen, Yadier Molina, and Jim Edmonds. The pitching staff was largely built around a bullpen that featured Wainwright and Jason Isringhausen. It didn't hurt to have a Hall of Fame manager, Tony La Russa, in the dugout, with longtime pitching guru Dave Duncan alongside.

The Mets had won 97 games in the regular season, but injuries to Pedro Martinez and Orlando "El Duque" Hernandez changed the dynamic of the team as the postseason dawned. And yet, none of it seemed to matter as the Mets were sweeping the Dodgers in the NLDS.

"The Mets had the best team in the regular season, but once they lost Pedro and El Duque right before the playoffs started they didn't have the best team anymore because they didn't have enough starting pitching," Gary Cohen said. "While that team if it had been intact certainly should have been the favorite to win it all, as it was constituted by the end of that NLCS it was not the same team."

The shift actually began in July, when right-handed reliever Duaner Sanchez was involved in an accident in South Florida. Sanchez, out for a late-night meal, was in a taxi that got sideswiped by a drunk driver and suffered a severely separated right shoulder. Suddenly, the Mets needed bullpen help, prompting Minaya to trade outfielder Xavier Nady to the Pirates for Perez and Roberto Hernandez.

"Duaner Sanchez had made my life and Aaron Heilman's life tremendously easy," Wagner said. "He was a dude. He was throwing the ball as well as anyone. He was an asset and then he gets hurt and he's done and it throws off your mojo a little bit. It just seems like there were always little things."

Even so, if Beltran could battle back against Wainwright, sending the Mets to Detroit for Game 1 of the World Series, it wouldn't matter that the bullpen had caved in a big spot, with Heilman surrendering a two-run homer to Molina in the ninth.

The previous batter, Floyd, had struck out on a sharp breaking ball the Mets were unaware was in the right-hander's arsenal.

"We didn't have a lot of information on Wainwright at the time," Floyd said. "He was a closer, so we had limited information, and that's how the game has changed. When we opened up the binder we had Waino's name in there because he was on the roster. As far as his out-pitch, a 12-to-6 breaking ball, that wasn't in there."

Floyd's hope was Beltran had gotten a good look at Wainwright's breaking ball from the on-deck circle.

"Carlos could actually hit backward, meaning he could sit on off-speed and still hit fastball," Floyd said. "I was hoping he sat on that breaking ball."

Peterson's prediction that Wainwright was about to unleash a breaking ball proved accurate: Beltran was mesmerized, taking a called third strike to end the series.

71

Billy Wagner's huge fastball, with a personality to match, brought a presence to the Mets bullpen and clubhouse from 2006 to '09. Wagner finished his major league career with 422 saves.

In later discussions with La Russa about the at-bat, Minaya found out the catcher Molina had cast aside the plan given to him by Duncan.

"Those pitches to Beltran were unhittable and the reality is there's not much you can do," Minaya said. "You are talking about a great competitor. The only thing I look at about that, watching Molina, he changed the sequence of the pitches. People forget about that. I thought the one thing that stood out in Game 7 besides the Endy Chavez catch was Molina changed the game plan they originally started with.

"Molina changed the sequence on his own, without the consent of the manager and the pitching coach, and it just told me how great Molina was. He was a young kid at the time."

After the numbing defeat, Floyd, Wright, and Paul Lo Duca were out at a nightspot in Manhattan's Meatpacking district trying to unwind from the game. The group was largely congratulated for a fine season, but not everybody shared the same view.

"Some fans had just left the game and they were chirping and obviously ticked off that we weren't going to the World Series, and you see how fights get started," Floyd said. "You see how things can escalate to something crazy. It got hairy for a minute, but then we just bounced. But you could see the city was just on fire. Everybody felt that was our year."

Wagner had contributed to the NLCS disappointment by surrendering a tie-breaking homer to So Taguchi in the ninth inning of Game 2. The Cardinals added two additional runs against Wagner in the inning and tied the series.

"I pitched all three games against Los Angeles and then the first two against St. Louis and I probably didn't have very much on anything," Wagner said. "But in that situation [against Taguchi], I could have dealt with him popping up or Endy jumping over the fence and making the catch then. There were so many things in that whole series that were just awesome. That whole very stressful series.

"I don't think anybody can understand what being in the playoffs is like unless you have been in New York. That is such an awesome, stressful, every emotional thing in the world situation. When I look back on those things and am talking to those kids today, it's 'You have no idea how easy this is, to be able to handle these things.' But that is why I came to New York."

The season ended without a World Series appearance, but to Minaya it was a success.

"I think the excitement of the season overrides the disappointment for me," Minaya said. "It was a fun group of guys, the fan base was energized, and the stadium was full. That being said, the ending was you came so close. A pitch here or a pitch there we missed, but overall it was a good memory. It was fun."

*　*　*

The Mets' transformation into a playoff team had started following the 2004 season with Minaya's arrival as general manager. Beltran and Martinez were signed as free agents as Wright and Jose Reyes continued to emerge as bright young stars. The following offseason Delgado and Lo Duca arrived in separate trades with the Marlins, giving the Mets an everyday lineup that could rival any in the National League.

The last needed piece was an electric closer to replace Braden Looper, who had been a disappointment in the role. Minaya went to the top of the free-agent market and signed Wagner to a four-year contract worth $43 million. At that point the left-hander had already accumulated 284 saves in a 10-year career with the Astros and Phillies.

Wagner was entering a new world in New York, one in which he would be compared to Yankees icon Mariano Rivera. Early controversy emerged when Wagner entered games at Shea Stadium to the beat of Metallica's "Enter Sandman"—a song that had become Rivera's trademark. Wagner also had been using the song for much of his career and wasn't about to relinquish it now. There was room in New York for two Sandmen, even if Rivera was clearly the standard by which all other closers were measured.

Randolph, who had served as a longtime Yankees coach before becoming Mets manager, wanted another Rivera.

"I think Willie wanted me to be Mariano more than I needed to be Mariano," Wagner said. "We had discussions about how he wanted me to be Mariano and I said, 'I do, too.' I wanted to be him, too, but there's some things you can't control. We all have to deal with the hand we're dealt, and I tried to explain that to Willie at times.

"As a young player you have to be humble enough to say, 'I'm not that guy. My numbers are good, I get who I am, but I am not who that is and I can't go out there and try to be something that I'm not.' It's like asking David Wright: 'Since you're the captain should everybody call you Captain, like Derek Jeter?' You come to a two-team city and you are going to get compared."

During his Mets tenure Wagner lived in Greenwich, Connecticut, near Glavine. The two began a carpool to Shea Stadium and used each other as a sounding board during difficult times. On days Glavine was scheduled to pitch, Glavine's wife, Chris, would sometimes bake cookies for Wagner and instruct the closer to help her husband get the win. Wagner came to appreciate Glavine's natural "glass-half-full" optimism.

For Wagner, the lowest point of that first season in New York came during the Subway Series on May 20, when he was summoned into a non-save situation, with his team ahead 4–0. Wagner retired only one batter and allowed four runs before the Yankees won the game in the 11th inning.

"The papers crushed me, I was getting blown up, all this stuff is going on, Willie is all over me and the next night I have to come out there, it's 4–3, and I have to get the save," Wagner said. "That's how you win fans. You come out there and you had that bad game and they are booing your ass, but you come out there and get the job done, that's how you win those things."

Driving to the ballpark with Glavine before that game, Wagner was as nervous as he had been in his major league career. In reflecting upon what had occurred in the previous game, Wagner blamed himself for mentally checking out with the four-run lead because he wasn't expecting to pitch. By the time he regained focus, it was too late. And failure had crept into his mind as the next game approached.

"I was like, 'Holy shit, what if I go out there and suck again?'" Wagner said. "So to come back the next day, that was a defining experience for myself on how the Mets fans are going to handle my having a bad game, and then coming back and getting it done."

The biggest adjustment for Wagner might have been learning to pitch on consecutive days after largely avoiding such workload demands during his tenure with the Astros and Phillies. To Wagner, the new blueprint felt like overuse, but Peterson was careful to ensure his closer was throwing the same number of innings—and even fewer pitches—as previously.

Wagner finished the season 3–2 with a 2.24 ERA and set a club record with 40 saves. It was a mark that stood for nearly a decade, until Jeurys Familia saved 43 games for the Mets in 2015.

"Billy was tough to deal with, but we always had an honest relationship and it was always straightforward and he always knew that I cared about him," Peterson said.

If anything, the pitching coach came to appreciate Wagner's forthrightness.

"If it came into Billy's mind, it came out of his mouth and you needed to understand that about Billy—he was truly shot with truth serum," Peterson said. "There were several times with several players that Billy was the person to put people back in line. He wasn't afraid to do that, and it really didn't matter who it was, but Billy was all about the team. It was all about winning."

* * *

The disappointment of 2006's near-miss was a picnic for the Mets compared to the following year.

"I think 'collapse' is a good word," Wright said. "We just crumbled down the stretch."

Up seven games on the Phillies in the NL East with 17 remaining, the Mets blew it in a meltdown of monumental proportions, culminating with a loss to the Marlins on the final day of the regular season.

The Mets bullpen was on fumes by September, with Wagner receiving regular shots because of back spasms. Heilman appeared in 17 games in the final month, taking on added burden with Wagner hurting.

Surrounding Wagner and Heilman was the cast of Pedro Feliciano, Jorge Sosa, and Scott Schoeneweis. Each was a specialist lacking the arsenal to endure a complete inning. The seeds of the September swoon may have been planted two months earlier, when the front office decided against adding another high-impact reliever and back-end starter. Pedro Martinez spent most of that season rehabbing a torn rotator cuff and didn't pitch his first game until September. The future Hall of Famer was solid in that final month, pitching to a 2.57 ERA in five starts, but working deep into games was an issue for Martinez, overextending a thin bullpen.

"You kind of felt it coming," Glavine said, referring to the collapse. "It just seemed like we could not get out of our own way. It was one of those situations where you would show up at the ballpark every night feeling good about what you were doing as a team and as the game started going along you just kind of sit there and say, 'What is going to happen tonight? How are we going to lose tonight?'

"Unfortunately for us, it happened in September, it didn't happen in June or July when we would have had time to recover from it. And it wasn't like, 'Hey, we need to hit better or we need to pitch better, we need to field better.' We needed to do everything better and it was just like every night it seemed like one aspect of our game just wouldn't be there."

Exacerbating matters, the sniping between Minaya's staff and the manager's office was constant, especially as the Mets' lead in the standings began to shrink. The freefall started with a Phillies three-game sweep at Shea Stadium beginning September 14 in which the Mets bullpen twice crumbled. Two straight losses in Washington followed, whittling the Mets' lead to 2½ games.

The Phillies weren't relenting, so even a burst in which the Mets won four of five games against the Nationals and Marlins failed to increase their lead in the standings. Adding to the hurts, Delgado was battling a strained oblique and played only 14 games in September.

John Maine's one-hitter against the Marlins on September 29 ended a five-game Mets losing streak and ensured the regular season finale the following day would have implications. If the Mets won, they would finish at least tied for the NL East lead.

The assignment fell upon Glavine, who earlier that season beat the Cubs at Wrigley Field for his 300th career victory. Glavine, at 41 years old, had pitched to a 4.14 ERA as a dependable middle of the rotation piece on a team that lacked a true ace. Glavine was undecided if he wanted to pitch in 2008, so it was possible the start against the Marlins would be the finale in his Hall of Fame career.

If there wasn't enough drama leading into the day, Wagner spent pregame trying to douse a *New York Magazine* story in which the closer said Randolph and Peterson were "not a lot of help" in dealing with the bullpen.

But the tone for the day, from Peterson's perspective, was set by leadoff batter Hanley Ramirez, in a meaningless game for the Marlins. Ramirez had 29 homers and 51 stolen bases as the day began.

"He needs one homer to join the 30-30 club, so we're talking about Hanley and I told Glavine, and he agreed, 'Just play the chase game,'" Peterson said. "He's going to swing. You can't hit a homer if you don't swing. Tommy started off 0–2 on Ramirez to lead off the game, and threw pitches just off the plate and Hanley is taking them."

Ramirez walked, the first domino in an unlikely chain of events. After two ground ball singles with one out, Cody Ross delivered a two-run double and scored on the play when Glavine's cutoff throw to third base sailed for an error. Two additional weak singles, a walk and a hit batter left the Mets in a 7–0 hole and Glavine was removed, having retired just one batter. The Mets lost 8–1, giving the victorious Phillies the NL East title by one game.

"My two or three starts leading up to that were not very good," Glavine said. "I knew I was not throwing the ball well. I knew going into that game where I was and I was hoping against hope that I was going to go out there and figure something out and I didn't. Some of it maybe they didn't hit some balls hard here and there, but at the same time I know I didn't pitch well and I'm not going to blame it on bad luck."

Glavine had never been totally embraced by Mets fans because of his long career with the enemy Braves, and his postgame comments following his team's loss in Game 162 may have forever sealed his legacy in New York.

A reporter asked Glavine about the devastation of such a loss.

"I'm not devastated," Glavine said. "I'm disappointed, but devastation is for much greater things in life. I'm disappointed, obviously, in the way I wanted to pitch. I can't say there is much more I would have done differently."

Wagner felt badly for the team and his friend Glavine, but also understood why Mets fans were ruffled by what seemed like apathy by the pitcher.

"He was just the consummate professional and consummate teammate and to go out in that situation like that, it's not befitting of a Hall of Famer," Wagner said. "I hated that for him because of what he meant to the Mets organization and the people in there. He was never going to rock the boat. But you really have to identify with the blue-collar Met fan who goes out there and says, 'Man, I have worked my ass off all day to come to this game, you go out there in the biggest game of the year and you suck.' And that's tough, but if you know Glavine he is never too high or too low."

Glavine says he still catches flak from Mets fans about his "not devastated" comment, but says he doesn't regret saying it.

"I think by saying that people somehow construed it as I didn't care, but that couldn't be further from the truth," Glavine said. "It's the only game in my career that I look at and say, 'God, I wish I could do that over,' because in my mind I had a wonderful experience in New York and in many regards that ruined it.

"I think we can all think of things in life that are devastating and I am not sure that losing a baseball game would qualify as being devastating. Rightly or wrongly that was probably me trying to put perspective into my own mind because I was pissed, I was embarrassed."

When Minaya considers the three-year stretch of 2006–08 in which the Mets had championship caliber teams but fell short, he doesn't hesitate in placing one season all alone.

"No doubt, '07 was the worst," Minaya said. "In '06 we didn't win, but at the end of the day we went far and got beat by the team that won the World Series. Those years we were always close to first place or in first place and '07 we were up seven with 17 to go. That was the heartbreaker."

Mike Vaccaro, the lead sports columnist for the *New York Post*, had witnessed an epic meltdown across town three years earlier when the Yankees lost four straight games against the Red Sox in the ALCS to become the first team in baseball history to blow a 3–0 series lead in the postseason.

It's open debate whether the Mets' 2007 meltdown belongs on the same level as the Yankees' collapse.

"One was just boom, boom, boom," Vaccaro said. "The other was just an awful 2½ weeks where every day bad stuff happened."

* * *

Randolph was a marked man following the 2007 collapse. Though the Mets had been banged up and also crippled by the front office's decision to stand pat at the trade deadline—rather than add a starting pitcher and reliever—Randolph shouldered much of the blame.

"I respect Willie as a person, but if you're going to have accountability as a manager, I just think there's some things he could have done differently in terms of how he set the tone and tried to manage the situation," said Adam Fisher, whose ascent in the Mets front office had started during Minaya's tenure.

"Obviously it got out of Willie's control. The way he handled it didn't work. When a team collapses that badly there are some real issues around leadership and everybody. From our standpoint I felt we could have given them better starting pitching, but that doesn't excuse the collapse, because there were plenty of chances to win a few games."

Minaya had selected Randolph as manager in part because of their shared New York City pedigree, growing up in the outer boroughs. That Randolph had won two World Series as a player with the Yankees and coached under Joe Torre as four additional world championship banners were raised in the Bronx only enhanced his status with Minaya.

"The reason I chose Willie was he was a New Yorker," Minaya said. "He cared. He showed passion. We knew the beat of the city and I thought Willie did a very good job. When you're from New York and you are from Queens and Brooklyn, you live the city. You live the season every day."

The Mets returned largely the same cast for '08, with the notable addition of Johan Santana to lead a starting rotation that had lacked a true ace the previous season. Santana arrived in an offseason trade with the Twins and immediately received a six-year contract worth $137.5 million, the largest deal in Mets history at that point. He would join a rotation that included Martinez, Maine, Oliver Perez, and Mike Pelfrey.

In June, with the Mets struggling, Randolph's hot seat was practically on fire. It became unclear if Randolph would survive a Father's Day weekend series, in which an omen may have occurred: Randolph's predecessor, Art Howe, had returned to Shea Stadium with the Rangers, for whom he was serving as bench coach. The Mets split a Sunday doubleheader with the Rangers, leaving their record at 33–35, and postgame rumors were swirling that Minaya had decided to fire Randolph and Peterson. With the bus outside the stadium waiting to carry the team to the airport for a flight to Southern California, the GM and manager convened in the hallway outside Randolph's office. Randolph asked Minaya multiple times if he should get on the bus, and was told he should.

"We get on the bus, we get on the plane and they are loading up the plane and I sit down next to Willie and say, 'Do you know what is going on?'" Peterson said. "If you know what is going on, do me a favor, I am getting off the plane, call Omar and he can call me at the beach tomorrow. I don't need to fly to fucking Anaheim for this."

Randolph assured Peterson he hadn't been told anything suggesting they were about to get fired. After the Mets beat the Angels 9–6 the following night, Peterson received a message as he was showering in the coaches' room that Minaya needed to speak with him back at the team hotel. Randolph, Peterson, and first base coach Tom Nieto were fired in separate meetings with Minaya, with the news breaking in New York at 3:14 AM, long after the final editions of the newspapers had gone to print. Bench coach Jerry Manuel was elevated to manager.

Manuel had previously managed the White Sox, and it was no secret he coveted Randolph's job. At one point, with the firing near, the *New York Post* ran a back page that photoshopped a knife into Manuel's hand as he stood behind Randolph's back.

Manuel, in temperament, was Randolph's polar opposite.

"Willie was heart on his sleeve and he managed with a competitive fire, and he wasn't as laid back as Jerry by any means," Wagner said. "Jerry had been that buffer coach on the bench, so he had a relationship with the players. As a manager you don't get to have that relationship with your players very often because there always is that uncomfortable moment you have got to have with those players about telling them they have to pick it up or we're getting rid of you.

"As the buffer coach it was easy for Jerry to transition in because he kind of knew the temperature of the team and what you need to do. I know he wanted to be the manager, like many of those guys did, but this was almost a tryout. He pretty much had a stacked team."

* * *

Within a month of the managerial change, the Mets moved into first place in the NL East. The team's firepower was impressive, matching up to the dangerous lineup the Phillies were fielding on a nightly basis, led by Ryan Howard, Jimmy Rollins, Chase Utley, and Jayson Werth. The Mets could counter with Carlos Delgado, on his way to a 38-homer season, with Wright, Reyes, and Beltran also performing at high levels. The Phillies placed Cole Hamels atop their rotation and the Mets had Santana.

Even with Wagner on the disabled list for almost all of August with a partially torn ligament in his left elbow, the Mets managed to hold the bullpen together with journeymen such as Luis Ayala and Brian Stokes.

Wagner's biggest confidant during his ordeal was Moises Alou, a former teammate with the Astros. The Mets signed Alou before the 2007 season, but the 40-year-old outfielder battled various ailments and struggled to stay on the field. In 2008 he played in only 15 games for the Mets. As Wagner contemplated trying to pitch through the partially torn ligament, Alou offered advice.

"He told me you can't worry about 'what ifs,'" Wagner said. "You have got to go out and got to do this and if it blows out it blows out. If it doesn't, you go out there and pitch."

The Mets, hopeful their star closer would return, received a gut punch in early September, when Wagner walked off the mound during a simulated game holding his elbow. He had fully torn his medial collateral ligament and would need Tommy John surgery.

"So I go out and blow out and [Alou] was the guy that when I woke up from surgery, he was there," Wagner said. "He was at my bedside at 6:30 in the morning. When you have teammates like that you knew you had done something right."

With Wagner out, the Mets' thin bullpen was pushed beyond the limit. Suddenly, the reinforcements began to wilt in the heat of a pennant race. The Mets led the NL East by 3½ games after beating the Nationals on September 10, but fell into second place over the next two weeks. Even so, the Mets remained in contention for both a division title and wild-card berth as the final weekend of the season approached against the Marlins.

Santana fired a gutty shutout on short rest on the penultimate day of the regular season, but the Phillies' victory over the Nationals mathematically eliminated the Mets in the NL East. Tied with the Brewers in the wild-card race, the Mets needed a Sunday victory to continue their season.

Adding to the drama, a postgame ceremony was scheduled to commemorate the final regular season game in Shea Stadium's history.

Across the parking lot, Citi Field was almost finished and would be open for business to begin the 2009 season.

Oliver Perez vanquished the ghost of Glavine by giving the Mets a respectable performance into the sixth inning, allowing only two runs. Beltran blasted a two-run homer for the Mets, tying it 2–2 in the sixth, but Wes Helms and Dan Uggla hit solo blasts against Scott Schoeneweis and Ayala, respectively, in the eighth and the Mets never recovered. The Brewers had already won, moving ahead in the wild-card race, by the time Ryan Church's shot to deep center was caught by Cameron Maybin for the final out in the Mets' season and the history of Shea Stadium.

"In 2008 I just don't think we had the firepower other teams had," Wright said. "We were piecing things together. Guys were hurt. [Wagner] was hurt. That year, CC [Sabathia] was pitching every second day it seemed for Milwaukee and we didn't have the firepower that other teams had that were in that group."

Amid the heartbreak of a second straight knockout on the final day of the regular season by the Marlins, the sellout crowd of 56,059 watched a procession of Mets heroes walk onto the field at Shea one final time. It culminated with Tom Seaver delivering a pitch to Mike Piazza, closing the ballpark.

"There was a lot of argument over whether they should have done the ceremony before the game, but I thought the ceremony afterward was perfect," Gary Cohen said. "You are closing the stadium. You don't close the stadium and then play a game, and if they had the ceremony and then go to the postseason, it wouldn't have had as much impact.

"But I think the ceremony became as heartbreaking as it was because of the circumstances of what had happened in the game. It was a fascinating range of emotions from the deflation of losing the game and processing that, to minutes later now this celebration of all the returning players...the range of emotions that afternoon was just like a roller coaster. Not the least of which was when Ryan Church hit that ball that ended the game, when it first left the bat I thought it might have a chance."

In the six seasons that followed, with the Mets relegated to playing meaningless September games (and often in August too), the collapses of 2007 and '08 would almost seem like the good old days.

"Look at the attendance, look at the SNY ratings, the franchise value, all those things, and we won a lot of games," Minaya said. "We just couldn't close it out. The stadium was a fun place and Mets fans want to win every year, but all the Met fan wants is to be able to play in September and be in meaningful games, and all those things were accomplished. We just did not accomplish winning. We got to the playoffs once [in 2006], but we should have been in the playoffs and World Series more times."

*　*　*

The misery for Mets fans was compounded in 2008 when the Phillies won the World Series, beating the Rays. Cliff Floyd, who had departed the Mets two years earlier, was a contributor off the bench for Tampa Bay's pennant winning–team and upon talking to a reporter as the postseason began, requested a keepsake before Shea Stadium was demolished by the wrecking ball.

"Maybe they can box up a rat and send it to me," Floyd said.

Jimmy Rollins had emerged as Public Enemy No. 1 among Mets fans for his sharp tongue and equally dangerous bat. In the offseason, he and Wright became teammates as members of Team USA in the World Baseball Classic. The manager was Davey Johnson, whose greatest glory had come in guiding the Mets to their 1986 World Series title.

Rollins and Wright bonded during their few weeks together, as Team USA advanced to the semifinals, losing to Japan at Dodger Stadium. It was Wright's walk-off single against Puerto Rico in a wild comeback victory in Miami that had allowed his team to advance. After the loss to Japan, Wright and Rollins were on a commercial flight together from Los Angeles to Atlanta. The breakup came with Rollins proclaiming "It's on again!" as the two players separated to catch connecting flights to their respective spring training destinations.

But for the Mets, it was never really "on" in 2009. Despite an active offseason that saw Francisco Rodriguez and J.J. Putz added to the bullpen and Perez re-signed to a three-year contract worth $36 million, injuries to Delgado, Beltran, and Reyes undermined a lineup that included 40-year-old Gary Sheffield in right field and Daniel Murphy attempting to learn left field. Putz was diagnosed with a bone spur and appeared in only 29 games for the team, pitching to a 5.22 ERA. He later indicated the bone spur was present when he pitched for the Mariners, but Mets doctors failed to detect it before he signed with the club.

Citi Field officially opened with the Mets' 6–5 loss to the Padres on April 13. The game's leadoff hitter, Jody Gerut, homered against Pelfrey, on a night Seaver was present to christen the team's new palace. Upon stepping into the spacious home clubhouse for the first time, Seaver remarked that he felt like he had entered the locker room at a country club. Sadly, Seaver had few appearances at Citi Field. The Hall of Fame pitcher's health became an issue in subsequent seasons, and in 2019 his family announced that Seaver had dementia and was retired from public life. The street outside Citi Field was renamed for Seaver later that year and plans were underway for the unveiling of a statue in his likeness. Seaver died at age 75 on August 31, 2020.

The Mets competed through the first two months of the 2009 season, but their spiral into the abyss began on June 12 in their first game at the new Yankee Stadium. Francisco Rodriguez, who had converted 16 of 16 save opportunities with his new team, got Alex Rodriguez to hit a pop-up to shallow right field for what would be the final out of a Mets victory. Rodriguez, in disgust, slammed his bat to the ground. The only problem for the Mets was Castillo dropped the ball, and by the time the relay throw from second base got to the plate the tying and winning runs had scored.

"You could see that play a thousand times and that would never happen," Derek Jeter said. "We stole a game."

Castillo's legacy with the Mets was cemented. Not only had the former All-Star second baseman lost a game by dropping a pop-up, but it had occurred in the spotlight of the Subway Series, where events are magnified tenfold. Just ask Dave Mlicki. The journeyman right-hander had a forgettable career, pitching to a 4.72 ERA over 10 major league seasons, but holds a special place in the heart of Mets fans for firing a shutout against the Yankees in the first regular season game between the rivals, on June 16, 1997.

Matt Franco was another relatively obscure Mets player whose tenure with the club is largely remembered for one Subway Series moment: he delivered a walk-off single against Mariano Rivera on July 10, 1999. The Mets won on walk-offs three times against the Hall of Fame closer in his career, with David Wright (2006) and Lucas Duda (2013) providing the other hits.

Castillo won three Gold Gloves in his career, but among Mets fans the mention of his name evokes only thoughts of ineptitude and a miscue that began the team's downfall in a season. In reality, injuries had cooked the Mets already.

"We were supposed to be the World Series champion," Minaya said, referring to a preseason *Sports Illustrated* cover. "But all of the injuries came together and that Castillo dropped ball was kind of the icing on the cake. There were so many things that happened that year. I thought we had a great team and we would be okay, but unfortunately that's not the way it went."

Minaya's decision to re-sign Perez looked bad almost from the start. The lefty returned from the WBC (he represented Mexico) out of shape, according to Mets pitching coach Dan Warthen, and never got on track. In 14 starts for the Mets he went 3–4 with a 6.82 ERA and continued to sputter the following year. In 2011, Perez and Castillo were released on the same day in spring training, after Minaya and Manuel had been fired the previous offseason.

"Some of those signings Omar ended up having, whether people got hurt or didn't perform, kind of sealed his fate," Jeff Francoeur said.

Among the few positive developments of the 2009 season was Wagner's return from Tommy John surgery, in August, after only an 11-month rehab. Such a fast return would be practically taboo within a few years, but Wagner's speedy comeback allowed the Mets to trade him to the Red Sox, for whom he would pitch in the postseason. In the off-season Wagner signed a one-year deal worth $10 million with the Braves in a farewell tour and went 7–2 with a 1.43 ERA and 37 saves. He retired after the 2010 season with 422 career saves.

Among pitchers who spent their career primarily as a reliever, only Hoyt Wilhelm, Dennis Eckersley, Rollie Fingers, Bruce Sutter, Goose Gossage, Trevor Hoffman, Rivera, and Lee Smith have been voted into the Hall of Fame.

"I would love to be there," Wagner said in 2019. "Do I think it will happen? I don't. Regardless of numbers, there is more to what's going on with guys, relievers going in, and I am glad for those guys. They are great. They are awesome. They brought a lot of attention to the role and they defined it and were the best at it.

"Being on the ballot is a tremendous accomplishment and I would love to be part of that game, but I am not holding my breath and I do enjoy the experience. If I had to sit there and build myself up, I just never have been that guy. I am not very good at it and I would probably shoot myself in the foot more than I would give myself a chance."

Wagner has embraced his new life as a high school baseball coach, even if it means dealing with parents harboring unrealistic expectations about their kids.

"As long as their kid plays and bats third, they don't care what happens, as long as they are on a winning program," said Wagner, who guided Miller School to state titles in Virginia in 2017 and '18. "The problem is I keep telling them you can't be on a winning program if you can't hit. It's awful hard to bat third if you can't hit. But it's fun. I enjoy the kids and it's fun to be around them and talk about reality."

* * *

One of the more bizarre incidents in the franchise's history occurred in the summer of 2009, during a press conference to announce that the team's director of player development, Tony Bernazard, had been fired. The decision to fire Bernazard was reached after a series of reports by Adam Rubin of the *New York Daily News* detailed Bernazard's erratic behavior around the organization's minor leaguers. Bernazard further buried himself by getting into a heated argument with Francisco Rodriguez on a team bus that escalated to the point witnesses thought a physical altercation might occur.

Among the incidents reported by Rubin was Bernazard had torn off his shirt during a postgame tirade and challenged players from Double-A Binghamton to a fight.

Bernazard, a former White Sox infielder, had become a lightning rod for controversy in the organization, as a known antagonist to Randolph before the manager was fired. Members of Randolph's staff became infuriated with a whisper campaign they believed was orchestrated by Bernazard.

"I just think it evolved to the point where they were fine in the beginning and then Tony just didn't respect Willie as a manager," Fisher said.

"It was one of those things that was just simmering under the surface. But Bernazard didn't get Willie fired. I think the whole front office was in agreement that a change was needed and the way they played under Jerry [Manuel] pretty much confirmed it."

A year later it was Bernazard who was finished with the Mets following an internal investigation that backed up Rubin's reporting. As Minaya sat at a podium at Citi Field to announce Bernazard's dismissal, the GM turned on the reporter.

"You have to understand this: Adam for the past couple of years has lobbied for a player development position," Minaya said. "He has lobbied myself, he has lobbied Tony."

Rubin sat flabbergasted in the back of the room, stung by the evident allegation he had conspired to get Bernazard fired. But Minaya denied accusing Rubin of such action.

"No, I am not saying that," Minaya said. "I am saying in the past, you have lobbied for a job.

"Over the years he said a number of times that he would like…he asked me personally to work in the front office. In my front office. Not only me, but he's asked others."

Minaya ultimately acknowledged his comments in the press conference were "inappropriate" and apologized to Rubin. Weeks later, with rumors flying that Minaya would be fired, Fred Wilpon made clear his intentions to retain the GM for the following season.

* * *

The 2009 season began a stretch in which the team's medical protocols were challenged, as Reyes, Beltran, and Delgado missed significant action and Santana was shut down in September to undergo arthroscopic knee surgery.

But the team's injury woes carried into 2010 and then would resurface during general manager Sandy Alderson's regime, sometimes with controversy attached.

"It was mostly bad luck and needing to improve communication, which I think can happen to any franchise," Fisher said. "Also, just communicating it to the media: we didn't have a great unified message. The Red Sox had similar injury issues that we did and didn't get the heat nationally that we did. They got the heat locally. Of course, the other thing is they won the World Series a couple of times. We had a huge confluence of events coming together. You have collapses. You have injuries, bad public relations, so all those things come into play."

If there was an incident that underscored that point, it was the concussion Ryan Church sustained with the Mets in 2008, when he took a knee to the head sliding into second base attempting to break up a game-ending double play. Church returned to action only two days later, and wasn't placed on the disabled list until after he had endured a flight to Colorado, worsening his post-concussion symptoms.

More than a decade later, Fisher defended the Mets' handling of the situation, to a degree.

"What people still don't understand is you can get on a plane with a concussion," Fisher said. "It wasn't necessarily handled well, but it wasn't handled nearly as poorly as sort of the urban legend has it. It took on a life of its own. We are still talking about Ryan Church's concussion 12 years later.

"They put him on a plane to go to Colorado and he started to have symptoms and everyone said, 'How can you put him on a plane,' because you think about pressure differences. But doctors say that doesn't have anything to do with anything. Could we have done a better job with the concussion protocol? Sure, but so could 30 NFL teams right now. I am not trying to make excuses. I am just saying we are trying to learn more and more about concussions, and from 2008 we are still evolving."

Ray Ramirez remained the team's trainer through the 2017 season and became a scapegoat for the Mets' injury troubles. Fisher scoffs at the notion Ramirez was the problem.

"Fans need somebody to blame," Fisher said. "I thought it was just lots and lots of things coming together."

CHAPTER 4
THE TEARDOWN AND REBUILD

Justin Turner is still trying to get over the Mets punting on a surprisingly competitive season.

It's several years after the fact, and Turner has emerged as an All-Star third baseman with the Dodgers after a nondescript Mets career as a utility infielder. He's at his locker in the home clubhouse at Dodger Stadium reflecting on the great friendships he formed with the Mets, but it's clear he was frustrated about the manner in which the organization was run.

"The hardest one for me was 2012; we were a few games out of first place going into the All-Star break and we had the worst bullpen in baseball," Turner said. "Maybe a couple of middle-leverage arms helps us play more meaningful games down the road and we basically had a meeting and were told, 'This is who we are, we are either going to win or lose with this group, we aren't making any trades.' We came out of the All-Star break and went [1–10], so I think looking back on that it was probably one of the harder things to deal with during that time.

"If we make a couple of moves for a couple of small bullpen arms and get some help down there, maybe we are playing meaningful games in August and September. That was disappointing because they were basically in a holding pattern, waiting for the cavalry, waiting for the Harveys and Wheelers and they didn't want to do anything. They didn't care if they won or lost basically because they were waiting for those guys."

These were lean payroll times for the Mets, in the aftermath of Bernie Madoff's Ponzi scheme in which team owners Fred Wilpon and Saul Katz had a reported $500 million invested at the time of Madoff's arrest in 2009. Suddenly, that money was gone, casting questions about whether Wilpon and Katz had the financial wherewithal to keep the team. Already, general manager Sandy Alderson—hired to direct a rebuild that wouldn't involve significant dollars—had traded Carlos Beltran and Francisco Rodriguez the previous year. And after 2011, the Mets took a passive approach with Jose Reyes and watched the

All-Star shortstop defect to the Marlins for a six-year contract worth $106 million.

Alderson, who had built Oakland's powerhouse teams that reached three straight World Series from 1988 to '90, was lured from the commissioner's office to oversee the post-Madoff madness. A payroll that had spiked around $140 million was slashed—at one point by almost 50 percent—and a team operating in the nation's largest market suddenly became more akin to the Milwaukee Brewers or Minnesota Twins than the crosstown Yankees.

"We were trying everything," said J.P. Ricciardi, the former Blue Jays general manager who was hired by Alderson as a special assistant in charge of finding major league talent. "Cripes, I signed Jason Isringhausen out of a workout. I worked him out and signed him that day and he ended up being a good guy in the bullpen, but we were basically like the Statue of Liberty: 'Give us your tired, your poor, your huddled masses.' We were scrambling.

"Unfortunately, I had been in that situation before with Toronto when you're at rock bottom and you've got to try to get any kind of player that is presentable and gives you a slight upgrade over what you have, so I knew the task we were undertaking, but when you start going through it and living it, it's really hard."

Ricciardi and Paul DePodesta had been recruited by Alderson to join incumbent assistant general manager John Ricco in the front office. A decade earlier DePodesta pushed statistical analysis in Oakland's front office, beginning the rise of "Moneyball." In the movie by the same name, DePodesta is played by actor Jonah Hill and given a different name.

Ricciardi had spent 2010 as an ESPN studio analyst after his ouster in Toronto and was set to join the Red Sox before the Mets hired him.

"It was a pretty good job with the Red Sox, but I go back a long way with Sandy," said Ricciardi, who held various player development and front office jobs with Oakland dating to the 1980s. "Out of loyalty to [Alderson] and knowing the task he had in front of him, I thought I could help him more than I could help the Red Sox at that point, so I decided to go with Sandy, more out of loyalty than anything."

The first job for the new front office was hiring a manager. Alderson interviewed Bob Melvin, Chip Hale, Wally Backman, and Clint Hurdle, among others, but ultimately chose their 61-year-old minor league field coordinator, who had flamed out in managerial positions with the Astros and Angels in part because of a high intensity that turned players against him.

Terry Collins at that point hadn't managed in the major leagues in 11 years, but was backed by DePodesta (who, as Dodgers GM, tried to hire Collins as manager but was rebuffed by ownership) and Fred Wilpon, who had a long relationship with Sandy Koufax, who had become close with Collins over the years. Collins had been a finalist for the Mets managerial job when Willie Randolph was hired six years earlier. After a stint managing in Japan, Collins became the Mets' minor league field coordinator in 2010.

The biggest question would be if Collins had the patience to preside over a rebuild, even as Alderson and team COO Jeff Wilpon were publicly stating intentions to compete for the playoffs. But Collins resolved to not put too much pressure on himself, hoping to avoid the burnout that had derailed him in previous managerial jobs.

"When I got hired I told myself to start enjoying the job," Collins said. "These jobs are hard to get and I know it's New York, I get all the competitive stuff, but Sandy was upfront: we're going to make some changes here, we are going to retool it a little bit, so there might be a couple of bumps in the road.

"But I was also a minor league guy, a development guy. So sometimes you have got to take a step back from winning and realize, 'We have got to get this guy better.' When you looked at the big picture of things, are we progressing in the areas with certain guys who are going to be here in three or four years? And that is what I kept telling the coaches: only worry about the guys who are in that clubhouse. That other stuff is not our job."

* * *

Collins faced no bigger hurdle than trying to resurrect Jason Bay, after the veteran outfielder had struggled through the previous season, the start of a four-year contract worth $66 million.

The Mets pursued Bay after deciding the top power-hitting corner outfield option on the market, Matt Holliday, would cost too much. There was also a resistance toward dealing with Holliday's agent.

"We were going to sign Jason Bay or Matt Holliday and we kicked them both around and Holliday had Scott Boras and Jason Bay had Joe Urbon as his agent," said Wayne Krivsky, a special assistant in the Mets front office from 2009 to '11. "It came down to we could get Jason Bay for 'X' and it was going to take 'X plus Y' to get Matt Holliday, not only in dollars, but in years. It was an organization decision that was unanimous, plus Boras was going to string you along to sign Holliday. We felt that Holliday was the better player overall, but for the value in the contract we were much more comfortable signing Jason Bay."

The 31-year-old Bay was twice an All-Star with the Pirates before hitting 36 home runs for the Red Sox in 2009. Team officials believed Bay's right-handed swing wouldn't be compromised by Citi Field's vast left-field dimensions because of his ability to pull the ball down the line. And the fact Bay had thrived in a media market like Boston told the Mets he had the makeup to handle New York.

But Bay's production dropped significantly upon arriving to the Mets in 2010. He had only six homers and a .749 OPS on July 25, when he became concussed after hitting the left-field fence chasing a flyball at Dodger Stadium. Bay missed the rest of the season.

The Mets' expectation was Bay would rebound in 2011, but it became clear by midseason that he wasn't the same player they had signed. Bay finished with 12 homers, and was booed regularly at Citi Field.

Bay's former teammate and still close friend Jeff Francoeur says multiple factors conspired to derail the slugger.

"I watched the game the other night and I saw Pete Alonso hit his 52nd homer and I watched J.D. Davis hit a home run to right-center," Francoeur said late in the 2019 season. "Both of those are doubles when we played here in the old Citi Field. I think about all the balls that I hit that got caught at the warning track or hit doubles off the wall. They are home runs now.

"Psychologically, it's different. He went to Boston and he would pop balls up to left field and they were doubles. Here they were outs and then that concussion in L.A. did a lot more damage than people ever realized, and I never believe Jason was the same after that concussion. One of the best teammates I ever had and I hated for it for him that it ended the way it did, because you saw him in Pittsburgh and Boston. We saw Jason Bay that was a real good left fielder. It just didn't work out here."

Bay became an afterthought in 2012, when he sustained a second concussion and finished with eight homers in 70 games. The Mets bought out the final year of his contract after the season.

"I just think [Bay] was a big fat snowball that was going downhill," said R.A. Dickey, who spent three seasons as Bay's teammate. "He worked his butt off, there was no lack of commitment, lack of work. He was a pro, too, after all that crap. I know everybody under the sun tried to identify what was going on offensively with him. He was always a great defender, even when he was struggling offensively."

* * *

The two biggest developments in Collins' first season were trades: at the All-Star break closer Francisco Rodriguez, who had a vesting option worth $17.5 million in his contract that kicked in based on appearances, was dealt to the Brewers. And then two weeks later Carlos Beltran was traded to the Giants for pitching prospect Zack Wheeler.

Beltran, playing out the seven-year contract worth $119 million he had received before the 2005 season, had a contentious relationship with the Wilpons. Much of that tension stemmed from Beltran's decision to undergo arthroscopic knee surgery before the 2010 season. The Mets said Beltran had the surgery without their consent, a charge Beltran's agent, Boras, denied. Later in the season the Mets attempted to publicly smear Beltran by leaking to the media that he was among the three players (Oliver Perez and Luis Castillo were the others) that skipped a team visit to Walter Reed National Military Medical Center outside Washington, D.C. On the morning of the visit, Beltran had a meeting for his foundation that provides opportunities for children in Puerto Rico.

With the Mets fading in the playoff race the following year, Alderson found a taker for Beltran: the Giants—who had won the World Series in 2010 and were gearing up in an attempt to repeat and willing to surrender Wheeler for the veteran outfielder.

"Times have changed between then and now," Wheeler said. "Most people wouldn't give up their top pitching prospect for a rental, so now that I look back it's kind of fun and weird, because it's not going to happen really anymore."

Rodriguez's trade to Milwaukee was strictly a salary dump. The emotional closer's defining moment with the Mets came the previous year, when he was arrested at Citi Field for assaulting his father-in-law in a team family area following a game. Rodriguez was placed in a holding area in the ballpark and booked. He was ordered by a judge to attend anger-management sessions.

"I think the one thing the Mets have learned, signing guys as it has gone on from there, is they have signed higher-character people," Francoeur said. "People they didn't have to worry about something like that happening anymore. It's been good."

As for Beltran, a short reunion with the Mets occurred before the 2020 season when he was hired to manage the team. Only 77 days into the job, before he had even managed his first game, he parted ways with the organization, after an MLB investigation named him as involved in the Astros' illegal sign stealing scheme in 2017.

To those around the Mets in Beltran's playing days, his return to the organization—for even a few months—would have seemed improbable. Francoeur recalled an anecdote from 2009 or '10 when Beltran was with the team rehabbing from an injury and decided to bake a cake.

"The guy can cook and he is passionate about it," Francoeur said. "After this one game he made a Tres Leches cake, it's my favorite desert. We came out of the game, we had won the game, too, so everybody was happy. Jeff [Wilpon] came in and said to Beltran, 'I am glad we are paying you $18 million to bake a fucking cake.' I always thought that was one of the funniest things I heard in my life, but the cake was worth every penny."

* * *

My first year covering the Mets full time for the *New York Post* was 2010, after spending the previous three seasons in a backup role, rotating between the two New York baseball teams. And that first season as Mets beat writer was maybe the most memorable, in part because of Francoeur, who had arrived the previous season in a trade with the Braves.

Francoeur—better known as "Frenchy"—was unfiltered, and his locker became a frequent hangout for writers looking for a funny quote. In a testament to his affability, Francoeur won the "Good Guy" award, voted on by the New York chapter of the Baseball Writers' Association of America, despite having played only the final two months of the 2009 season for the Mets. The award annually goes to the Yankees or Mets player who is most cooperative with the media.

Francoeur's responsibilities for the Mets, besides playing the outfield, included organizing the daily card game. Francoeur, Bay, and David Wright were among the everyday players, but a rotating cast filled the table.

"David was a good poker player and Louie Castillo was by far the worst," Francoeur said. "You could take Castillo's money in two seconds. He stayed in, every hand. He never saw a hand he didn't like."

Francoeur's enduring memory of his Mets tenure was his only Opening Day with the organization. The previous year, *Sports Illustrated* had put the Mets on the cover and picked them to win the World Series, but injuries decimated the team, eliminating it from the postseason race early.

"I still laugh when I think about Opening Day in 2010," Francoeur said. "Three people got booed during the introductions: the two trainers and Oliver Perez. It's the only place I have ever been where the trainers got booed. Unbelievable. I have seen players, but trainers? Opening Day?"

Francoeur was traded later that season and ended up in the World Series with the Rangers. He spent most of his career bouncing around the NL East, returning to the Braves after playing for the Phillies. Francoeur ended his career in 2016 with the Marlins.

Late in Francoeur's final season, teammate Jose Fernandez and two other men were killed when the boat Fernandez was determined to be driving smashed into a rock jetty in the Atlantic. According to a toxicology report, Fernandez had cocaine in his system. Francoeur had been invited on previous occasions to ride with Fernandez in the boat, but declined.

"The last week of my life in the big leagues was Jose Fernandez's death," Francoeur said. "Honestly, there aren't many days that go by where you don't think about it."

In a somber scene in Miami, the Mets were the opponent for the Marlins' first game following Fernandez's death. Dee Gordon homered leading off the game for the Marlins on what Francoeur suspects might have been a grooved pitch by Bartolo Colon.

"That is why I love him," Francoeur said, referring to Colon. "He's the best because of that. Whether he grooved it or not, I thought it was a cool moment and it was tough because the Mets were still working on the wild card, they had the lead, but it wasn't clinched yet and I always said I thought it was really impressive how Terry [Collins] and the entire Mets team handled the situation. It was really cool."

Francoeur became an analyst on TBS' postseason coverage in 2019, bringing his insights to a national audience. He still speaks regularly with Wright, whom he considers a close friend.

"The important thing is just the way I played the game and the teammates I made and the relationships," Francoeur said. "I think it's a lot of the reason I am able to do what I am doing now."

* * *

Dickey was a player the Mets had plucked from the scrapheap before the 2010 season with the idea the veteran knuckleballer could bring organizational depth as a spot starter or long reliever. Dickey was 35 years old and had struggled in his seven major league seasons, pitching for the Rangers, Mariners, and Twins.

He was born without an ulnar collateral ligament in his right elbow—a fact that was discovered after he was drafted by the Rangers, costing him most of an $810,000 signing bonus. Dickey had come close to quitting baseball on multiple occasions. If the Mets weren't his last gasp at establishing himself, they were certainly close to it.

The intrigue of Dickey's knuckleball made him a low-risk gamble worth taking in the eyes of Mets officials.

"Omar [Minaya] had chased me for a couple of years before I signed with Minnesota," Dickey said. "And he was real honest upfront. He said, 'It's a real longshot for you to make the team; just come to camp and show the big league guys what you can do.'"

With a crowded rotation that included Johan Santana, Mike Pelfrey, John Maine, and Perez, it was understood Dickey would begin the season at Triple-A Buffalo. But only a few weeks into the season Dickey had the kind of performance he needed to receive notice in Buffalo: he surrendered a single leading off the game and then retired the next 27 batters. Dickey had pitched the final game of his minor league career.

And for 2010 and '11, he emerged as a dependable piece in the Mets rotation, including a 2.84 ERA in his first season with the club.

In 2012, little that occurred in the first two months suggested Dickey was on his way to a historical season. That all changed in June, beginning with a start against the Cardinals the day after Santana threw the first no-hitter in franchise history.

"And I remember thinking to myself: 'This could be a big letdown because we poured so much energy into that game emotionally that we could arrive to the park, myself included, and be a bit drained,'" Dickey said.

Dickey threw a shutout, the first of five starts that month in which he didn't allow an earned run. Included were consecutive one-hitters against the Rays and Orioles. He was selected to the National League All-Star team and became the focal point of a Mets rotation that had surprisingly helped keep the team afloat in the playoff race.

But without a bullpen, the Mets folded in the second half. By September, only Dickey's pursuit of 20 wins and the Cy Young award mattered.

Dickey became emotional years later in recounting the day he won his 20th game, beating the Pirates at Citi Field in his final home start.

"We were out of the race and people were still coming out," Dickey said in 2019 with emotion in his voice, as if holding back tears. "I just remember all of it. I can almost remember every pitch that I threw in that ballgame. I didn't know at the time it was going to be my last [home start] for the Mets ever. I didn't really think of that part. I thought I was just going to come back."

Dickey finished 20–6 with a 2.73 ERA and led the NL with 230 strikeouts in becoming the third Mets pitcher, joining Tom Seaver and Dwight Gooden, to win a Cy Young award.

The knuckleballer had completed his two-year contract worth $7.8 million that contained a club option for 2013 and began seeking a new deal. But Dickey's contract situation also took a backseat to David Wright, who was eligible to hit free agency after the following season. With Christmas approaching, Wright received an eight-year contract from the Mets worth a club-record $138 million. The realization hit Dickey that the Mets probably weren't going to give out another significant contract that winter.

"David had just signed an enormous deal and I knew that needed to be the priority for them," Dickey said. "When they were doing that Sandy was being honest with me how it was really tight [financially] and they were trying to figure out how it was going to work."

The answer was in a trade.

* * *

Catcher had been a Mets weakness for several seasons, and that point was underscored in 2012 when the Mets were using the likes of Josh Thole, Rob Johnson, Mike Nickeas, and Kelly Shoppach behind the plate. If the Mets weren't going to give Dickey a new contract, they could potentially use him to pry catching prospect Travis d'Arnaud from the Blue Jays.

In dealing with Toronto, it helped that Ricciardi was only three seasons removed from his post as the team's GM, and Mets scouting director Tommy Tanous also had recent Blue Jays roots. If the Mets were going to trade Dickey for d'Arnaud, they also wanted a second quality prospect in return. Pitchers Aaron Sanchez and Noah Syndergaard were the two names discussed.

"They didn't want to give up Sanchez," Alderson said. "They didn't think Syndergaard was going to develop a breaking ball. We were very happy to take Syndergaard, but it wasn't like he was a focal point of the deal. But he was definitely a player we recognized."

Ricciardi recalls a disconnect between the Mets and Blue Jays that he helped bridge. Toronto's GM was Alex Anthpoulos, who had served as Ricciardi's assistant with the Blue Jays.

"The interesting thing about that was Sandy saying, 'I can't get any traction with Alex,'" Ricciardi said. "So I would call Alex and he was telling me, 'I can't get any traction with Sandy.' So I felt like Henry Kissinger: I was getting the Arabs and Jews together. I kept telling Sandy, 'We can make this trade, let's just make sure we talk about this.' I would talk to Alex and say, 'Stay with this, Sandy wants to make this trade.' I was kind of the intermediary behind the scenes, telling Alex what to talk about, telling Sandy what to talk about or suggesting what they talk about and they were able to finish it off."

The final deal sent Dickey, Thole, and Nickeas to the Blue Jays for d'Arnaud, Syndergaard, veteran catcher John Buck, and minor league outfielder Wuilmer Beccera.

Before the trade was completed, Dickey reached an agreement with the Blue Jays on a two-year contract extension worth $25 million on top of his 2013 option. For Dickey, it was a bittersweet moment.

"It felt like it made a lot of business sense for them to try to capitalize on the year I had and get as much as they could, that made sense to me just from a logic standpoint," Dickey said. "I was sad about it because that was the team I resurrected my career with and had such great memories, my family did, too, and I love the fan base."

Dickey spent four years with the Blue Jays before pitching a final season in 2017 for the Braves. He retired with $57.6 million in career earnings, almost all of it coming after age 35, when he landed with the Mets as a journeyman just hoping to secure a major league job.

Long after his departure from the Mets, Dickey—who has retired to a farm in Nashville—still gets recognized when he visits New York City.

"I will go back there on a college visit with my daughter or walk in the city, because I just love the city, and I will run into 15 people that remember the way it was," Dickey said. "I have a pretty recognizable kind of face and beard, but I think it's just kind of those fans are devout.

"If you do well in New York you can go back to New York the rest of your life, that is just the way it is. Whereas Jason Bay would probably never set foot back in New York City ever again. There is no in between. It's just a different animal.... I can go back and feel a sense of appreciation, and that's nice for me. If I go back to Minnesota, nobody would recognize me."

As a young player, Dickey formed a bond with Mickey Callaway, who would manage the Mets for two seasons beginning in 2018. The two lived together while playing for the Rangers, but they had known of each other since high school.

Callaway starred at Germantown High in Memphis, which faced Dickey's team from Montgomery Bell Academy of Nashville in the 1993 Tennessee Class AAA championship.

"[Callaway] was a great pitcher, but he was hurt and he could only pinch-run in that game," Dickey recalled. "He was as fast as lightning. The guy could do a 360 dunk—just an incredible athlete. He was

Germantown's fastest player and they would pinch-run him. When I was pitching in the state championship it was 1–1 and they put him in to pinch run in the seventh. He stole second, stole third, and was three-quarters of the way down to home plate and got back safely to third base."

Dickey's team won the championship. The two pitchers then went to competing SEC schools, with Dickey at Tennessee and Callaway at Ole Miss.

When Callaway was hired to manage the Mets, one of his early calls was to Dickey, who had started 31 games for the Braves the previous season. The Braves had asked Dickey about returning on a club option for 2018, but the knuckleballer decided to retire. Callaway later called just to gauge Dickey's interest in a potential return to the Mets. But Dickey went through with retirement.

"It was hard to say no to the option money [with Atlanta], but so much of it was I spent a year watching Jose Bautista, for instance, just kind of bounce around from one team to the next after being an absolute titan in Toronto and he kind of limped out," Dickey said. "I didn't want to do that. I don't know if that is selfish or what, but I wanted to be able to end knowing that it ended well. That's why I kind of laid it down, and also because I had four kids 16 and under and I had missed the majority of their lives, so I am tending a farm in Nashville."

* * *

Alderson's desperation to find a relatively low-cost closer led him to signing veteran Frank Francisco before the 2012 season. The right-hander was best known for throwing a folding chair into the stands, breaking a woman's nose, when he pitched for the Rangers.

Francisco was almost an immediate disappointment for the Mets, but his tenure with the club is mostly remembered for a comment he issued to the *New York Post* before the start of the Subway Series against the Yankees. In the clubhouse at Citi Field two days before the start of the series, Francisco blurted out: "I can't wait to face those chickens. I want to strike out the side against them. I have done it before." When asked for an explanation, Francisco, perhaps already regretting his words, declined to elaborate.

The ambiguous comment ended up on the front page of the *Post*, with Derek Jeter's head transposed onto the body of a chicken. The headline screamed CLUCK YOU. When Francisco arrived to the clubhouse that day, a copy of the front page was on his chair, and from across the room, Justin Turner began blaring a version of the "Chicken Dance" on his iPod. Reliever Tim Byrdak took the show a step further by buying a live chicken in Chinatown for $8 and bringing it into the clubhouse. Byrdak named the chicken "Little Jerry Seinfeld"—a reference to an episode of the sitcom *Seinfeld* in which Kramer buys a rooster and gives it that name.

"At first I told [Francisco] the Yankees sent it over for him—he had a look of concern on his face," Byrdak said. "And then he said, 'You bought it.' And I said, 'Yeah, I bought it.' Everyone got a good chuckle out of it."

Francisco finally explained himself, saying the chicken comment related to the Yankees' habit of complaining about calls by the umpires.

Nick Swisher was the only Yankees player visibly annoyed by Francisco's words.

"I don't even know this dude and I don't think he knows any of us," Swisher said. "Those are some big words."

Little Jerry Seinfeld was sent to an upstate farm after the Yankees won two of three games in the series.

"Not too bad for a bunch of chickens," Swisher said.

Francisco went on the disabled list before the final game of the series with a strained oblique. It was the first setback of an injury-plagued two-year stint with the Mets. After the season Francisco underwent surgery to remove a bone spur from his elbow, and spent most of the year sidelined.

In spring training, Francisco had given me tips for losing weight that included drinking a certain kind of herbal tea. Upon returning to the team in September, after a five-month hiatus, the reliever's first words to me were, "You haven't improved."

Sadly, neither had Francisco. He was largely ineffective in his return and lasted only four games for the White Sox the following year before he was released, ending his major league career.

* * *

The Mets fared much better in their search for a low-cost bullpen veteran for 2013. But first, Alderson had to convince LaTroy Hawkins to accept a minor league deal. Hawkins, who already had pitched 18 big league seasons, was contemplating retirement if he didn't receive a major league contract.

"I was a little pissed off because the Mets was the only deal I had," said Hawkins, who had gone 2–3 with a 3.64 ERA for the Angels the previous year. "I talked to Sandy and was like, 'Okay, I'll sign [a minor league deal], but I was looking for more money. He said, 'Take it easy. I don't want to have to make a decision during that season that is going to affect you because of the money you are making.' I remember him telling me the more money I made, the greater chance there was a decision was going to be made during the season to let me go or not."

If the Mets had one thing to excite them in 2013, it was the organization's top pitching prospect, Matt Harvey, who had looked sharp after arriving to the big leagues for the final two months of the previous season.

Harvey's moniker, the "Dark Knight," was born following a *Sports Illustrated* cover story that gave him the nickname. And Harvey would fast become a fixture in the tabloid gossip columns for his active night life and appetite for dating models. He was already on record in a magazine interview as saying he wanted to be the next Derek Jeter in that regard.

Hawkins remembers having early concerns that the kid from southeastern Connecticut could block out potential distractions.

"I just thought him being from the East Coast would keep him from reaching his full potential, just because he was from that area," Hawkins said. "The distraction of being an East Coast guy playing in the city, it's not an easy thing to do."

Terry Collins tried his best to keep the 24-year-old's focus in the right place.

"I spent hours with Harvey," Collins said. "I loved him like a son. I was there when he first signed in the minor leagues. I was there when he first got to the big leagues, when he became a star. I tried to get him to understand what it took to stay a star: don't get caught up in the spotlight.

"The spotlight is going to be there, but you are going to be judged by what you did on the field, so that has to be the focus. Continue to do the stuff on the field. There were just some other things he got caught up with. We tried to tell him, 'In 10 years when you are a multi, multi-millionaire, go have all the fun you want.'"

Harvey was on his way to starting the All-Star game at Citi Field that season, and by mid-June, the Mets had Zack Wheeler ready for his major league debut. It came as part of a "Super Tuesday" doubleheader in Atlanta in which Harvey dominated in the first game and Wheeler took the nightcap. The Mets' future had arrived.

Wheeler tried to avoid any comparisons, because at that point Harvey was the clear alpha in the rotation.

'[Harvey] had his thing going on and I was just up there trying to mind my business and stay in the big leagues, so I really wasn't worried about [comparisons]," Wheeler said. "But I made a lot of good friends that year and a lot of guys showed me the ropes and made it pretty easy for me."

The bombshell arrived in August, when the Mets made public the results of an MRI exam on Harvey's right elbow: the pitcher had a torn ligament and would need Tommy John surgery. The prognosis called for Harvey to miss the next season.

Suddenly, the Mets' chances of taking a leap into the playoffs in 2014 appeared doomed. And then there were the questions of whether Harvey would return as the same pitcher in 2015.

"I kind of feel like it happens to everybody now," Wheeler said, referring to Tommy John surgery—he would undergo the procedure in 2015. "But as big as [Harvey] was here at the time and the persona, it stinks to have that happen."

The Mets finished the season with a rotation that included Wheeler, Jonathon Niese, Dillon Gee, and Daisuke Matsuzaka. Reports had begun to surface during the season about a pitcher named Jacob deGrom, whose raw stuff was impressing team officials in the minors, even if his numbers didn't show it.

And the Mets had been pleased with the development of Syndergaard, who split the season between Single-A St. Lucie and Double-A Binghamton. Syndergaard years later would reflect on his half-season in Binghamton as maybe the most fun he's had in baseball.

"I had a great time in Binghamton and have a special place in my heart for that town," Syndergaard said. "Just the overall city itself and the guys I was around. I felt that was an older team and I was close with a lot of the guys. The pitching staff was a tight-knit group and there was tons of ball-busting all around."

Later, Syndergaard would play for the Mets with many of those Binghamton teammates, names such as Erik Goeddel, Logan Verrett, Jack Leathersich, and Darin Gorski who would shuttle between the minors and big leagues to provide bullpen help. Goeddel became the most established of the group as a key contributor from the bullpen.

Hawkins, on his minor league deal that paid him only $1 million, remained with the Mets for the entire season and was among the top bargains of Alderson's tenure. The right-hander finished the season with a 2.93 ERA and 13 saves, becoming the closer late in the year.

Previously, Hawkins had pitched for the Yankees, giving him rare insight into the differences between the New York clubs.

"The Mets are just more laid-back," Hawkins said. "Everything is not 'Mets, Mets, Mets,' like it is 'Yankees, Yankees, Yankees.' Everything is about the Yankees over there from the TV you watch in the clubhouse, it's all about the Yankees. For homegrown Yankees that is cool for them, but for guys coming over it's a little different. The Mets were nothing like that. There was less force-feeding of their history."

Hawkins was embroiled in a controversy upon arriving to the Yankees in 2008 when he chose No. 21. The uniform had last been worn by Paul O'Neill, a key component of the Yankees teams that won four World Series titles in five years. Suddenly, Hawkins was faced with questions about his decision to wear O'Neill's number.

"Can you believe that?" Hawkins said. "You would have thought I took Yogi Berra's number. I still don't understand that. I mean, 'Hey, take it easy, that number is not going to the Hall of Fame. That number is for whoever wants to wear it.'"

* * *

Turner was driving to San Diego, about to represent the Mets at a Players' Association meeting following the 2013 season, when he received a phone call informing him he had been non-tendered by the club.

A 28-year-old infielder, Turner had slashed .280/.319/.385 in a backup role for the Mets and expected to return.

"Standing up in that Players' Association meeting and introducing myself, 'Justin Turner, I just got non-tendered an hour ago,' wasn't fun," Turner recalled in 2019.

The Mets, and the rest of baseball, couldn't have foreseen what was coming next. Turner signed a minor league deal with his hometown Dodgers and suddenly became a force. He hit .340 in his first year with the Dodgers and then improved his launch angle, averaging 21 homers over the next three seasons, which included an All-Star appearance in 2017.

"He basically came out of nowhere like a J.D. Martinez, but I don't think that would have happened with us, just because we didn't have the same playing opportunity," Alderson said, before conceding that David Wright's spinal stenosis that shortened his career might have provided an opening for Turner. "But I am happy for Justin, we didn't see that.

"There was another trade we made, right after my first year, Angel Pagan, and he went off with the Giants, good for him, so there were a couple of those that got away. But I don't think in Turner's case it was foreseeable, because actually Omar [Minaya] had claimed him off waivers from the Orioles the year before I got there, so this was a guy who had bounced around."

Wayne Krivsky was actually the driving force behind Turner landing with the Mets, after a stint with the Orioles. Krivsky had just arrived to the Orioles' front office in 2008 as a special assistant when he was asked to help complete a trade with his former team, the Reds, who had fired him as general manager earlier in the year.

The Orioles were trading catcher Ramon Hernandez to the Reds for utilityman Ryan Freel and players to be named later. As somebody who knew the Reds' farm system, Krivsky was asked to recommend players to Orioles general manager Andy MacPhail who would complete the deal. Krivsky didn't have to give the list of supplemental players a second look.

"And I said, 'Andy, I have got to tell you: Go get Justin Turner,'" Krivsky said.

The following season, Krivsky was working under Minaya with the Mets and happened to be in the office the day Turner was placed on outright waivers by the Orioles.

"I told Omar that we had to grab Justin Turner, the Orioles were making a mistake," Krivsky said. "This guy could do some things, he could hit, he was versatile. He could play all over the diamond and he was a very instinctive baseball player. That is how he ended up with the Mets."

Krivsky was a Twins special assistant when Turner got non-tendered by the Mets and tried to convince GM Terry Ryan to sign the player. Such a move would have required the Twins putting Turner on the 40-man roster, causing Ryan to hesitate.

By this time, Turner had almost come to expect ending up in the same organization as Krivsky.

"I called Justin in that period when he was a free agent and told him I was back with the Twins," Krivsky said. "He says, 'Should I get my red and blue spikes ready?' It turns out that we didn't free up a roster spot. Terry Ryan had a tough call to make, and regrets it today."

Turner was a popular player in the Mets clubhouse and wasn't shy about voicing his opinions, even jabbing team COO Jeff Wilpon in front of spectators on a back field at spring training. Turner had arrived early to camp for workouts—paying his own way—and Wilpon questioned why he wasn't wearing the same garb as his teammates.

"I had an orange shirt and everybody else had a blue shirt on," Turner said. "I made some smart comment like, 'You're not paying me to be here, I am going to wear what I want to wear. As soon as I am supposed to be here, on your dime, I will wear whatever you want me to.'"

During the season, Turner would receive occasional phone calls from Wilpon.

"He asked me to change my walk-up music, because I think his daughter wanted to hear certain songs," Turner said, noting that he complied. "The boss tells you to do something, and it's hard to say no."

* * *

It was easy to label 2014 as the most uninspiring Mets season in the second decade of the 21st century. Team expectations were low, as Harvey would spend the season rehabbing from Tommy John surgery and the organization continued to avoid pursuing high-end free agents. Veterans Curtis Granderson and Bartolo Colon were signed to provide a sense of stability.

An unexpected gift arrived in May, when Jacob deGrom was called up from Triple-A Las Vegas to work from the bullpen. DeGrom had impressed the organization's talent evaluators with his plus-fastball, but the 25-year-old right-hander arrived without significant fanfare. At the time, the Mets were awaiting Syndergaard and believed Rafael Montero could be a potential piece in their rotation.

DeGrom had spent the previous season pitching at three levels in the minor leagues and says he had "no clue" what he might become.

"You look at the year before I got called up, my Double-A numbers were not very good," said deGrom, who was 2–5 with a 4.80 ERA in 10 starts for Binghamton in 2013. "In '14, I started the year in Triple-A and was throwing the ball well. There were some guys that I felt were probably ahead of me. I didn't think I would get called up that early and didn't really know what I was."

The athletic 6'4" deGrom had initially played shortstop at Stetson University in Florida. After receiving an occasional opportunity to pitch from the bullpen, he became the team's closer his junior year. Four months after the Mets selected him in the ninth round of the 2010 draft, deGrom underwent Tommy John surgery, costing him the entire next season.

On May 12, 2014, deGrom arrived to the Mets and was told by manager Terry Collins he would pitch from the bullpen. But before that became a reality, Dillon Gee strained a lat and was placed on the disabled list. The Mets needed a starter in the Subway Series at Citi Field and gave deGrom his shot. On the biggest of regular season stages, deGrom allowed one run on four hits and two walks over seven innings. The Mets lost 1–0, but their rookie pitcher's stuff and composure was the buzz in the days that followed.

"Getting called up and saying I was going to be in the bullpen, I was real nervous about that because I hadn't thrown out of the bullpen my entire career," deGrom said. "The thing happened where Dillon got hurt and I got a chance to start, so I was very fortunate to be in the right place at the right time.

"Montero was going to be a starter and then I was going to be in the pen. That was interesting, trying to figure out that situation, and I remember after that game in Yankee Stadium, Terry called me in and said, 'You are going to start the second game at Citi Field.' That was a little bit of a relief for me because I knew my routine and felt comfortable with it and was just trying to go out there and prove I could pitch in the big leagues—to myself and the team as well."

DeGrom stayed in the rotation for the season's remainder and finished 9–6 with a 2.69 ERA and 144 strikeouts in 140⅓ innings. After the season he was named National League Rookie of the Year, joining Tom Seaver, Jon Matlack, Darryl Strawberry, and Dwight Gooden among Mets to win the award.

Suddenly, the Mets had the pieces for a dominant rotation. Harvey would be returning to pitch the next year, with Syndergaard on the horizon and Zack Wheeler showing signs he could be a dependable middle-of-the rotation pitcher. Steven Matz arrived behind Syndergaard, giving the Mets a "Fab Five" that was expected to carry the team into the 2020s.

But the most talented of the group, Harvey, didn't even have a job when 2020 began. His return from Tommy John rehab preceded surgery for thoracic outlet syndrome, and the Mets finally gave up on him in 2018, trading him to the Reds for catcher Devin Mesoraco. Harvey bounced to the Angels and Athletics the following year and was largely a disappointment. He tried another comeback, with the Royals in 2020, and pitched to an 11.57 ERA in seven appearances.

"Especially as a pitcher, you just never know," deGrom said. "That is why I say I'm thankful every day I can put this uniform on and do this, because you just never know when your time could be up as far as playing. The main thing is to try to stay healthy. It's easier said than done.

"There's some things that are out of your control, like nobody knows much about thoracic outlet and then Harvey gets it and you do the surgery and you just don't know. There's so many things that are unknown."

It wasn't until Harvey's final weeks with the Mets that the heralded five pitchers got to take a turn in the same rotation together. Whether it was Wheeler's Tommy John surgery, Matz's shoulder bone spur issues, Syndergaard's torn lat, or deGrom's elbow surgery, getting the group together was a challenge.

"That was always the thing that was always talked about: 'The five of you are going to run out there,' and it felt like it never happened," deGrom said.

DeGrom emerged as the best of the group, winning consecutive Cy Young awards in 2018 and '19. But the pitcher insists there wasn't a "eureka" moment along the way in which he knew he had arrived as a dominant force.

"I don't think there was ever a point, because I think even how I view it today, I'm still trying to figure out a way to get better," deGrom said in 2020.

"In 2016 I had my [ulnar] nerve moved in my elbow and I pitched with lesser velocity, but still had a decent year. I think still to this day, every year is different. You don't know how you are going to feel. You go into the offseason feeling good. But you don't know how you are going to come in feeling, so it's constantly working on getting back to where you were and then realizing what you need to do to get ready."

The vocal, colorful Syndergaard is deGrom's opposite in personality, but the two became friends and admirers of each other's talents. When deGrom sought a long-term contract, Syndergaard spoke up publicly urging the Mets to pay the pitcher. DeGrom ultimately received a five-year extension worth $137.5 million.

"I feel like earlier in deGrom's career nobody gave him the credit he deserved just in terms of the ability he possessed, but that is just how he is," Syndergaard said. "His walkup song is 'Simple Man' and the nickname on his jersey is 'Jake.' In a world where you see other sports personalities becoming super strong and defiant, he stays the same, stays under the radar.

"But I think now after the Cy Youngs, people are like, 'He's pretty freakin' good.' The competitive edge, the mental edge that he has, it's one to definitely admire."

For all his flamboyance, Syndergaard arrived to the major leagues speaking in hushed tones, especially around the media. In his early seasons with the club, the self-conscious Syndergaard preferred to hold his postgame interviews outside the clubhouse. The early perception was he had been intimated by Harvey, who had once chastised Syndergaard for conducting a group interview at his locker on a day he wasn't even pitching. But Syndergaard says it was just a "personal preference" to move his interviews outside the clubhouse.

"Still to this day I don't like all that attention and necessarily people hearing my thoughts as they are coming out, especially people I am close with," Syndergaard said. "I don't even want my parents to hear me doing interviews, to be honest. But I do remember [Harvey], he was busting my balls because I didn't even start that day, but everyone wanted to ask me questions about maybe the following day or something else."

Syndergaard was elated when Wheeler received a free-agent windfall from the Phillies after the 2019 season, even amid the disappointment of losing a friend in the Mets rotation. Syndergaard's emotions swing in the opposite direction when considering Harvey's career demise by age 30.

"I'm pretty bummed to see what happened to him because of the talent that he's possessed and it's hard to see somebody go from the tippytop of the world to coming down to the bottom," said Syndergaard, who missed the 2020 season after undergoing Tommy John surgery. "But I have always wanted the absolute best for him and to see him thrive and just be happy."

* * *

As the Mets' sixth straight losing season concluded in 2014, the team needed a new hitting coach. Dave Hudgens, who was hired by Alderson four years earlier, had been fired during the season and the Mets saw an opportunity to add a former Yankees coach with a strong resume.

From the franchise's inception in 1962, the Mets had never been shy about looking toward Yankees success in filling key positions. Casey Stengel, after presiding over seven Yankees World Series titles, was hired as the Mets' first manager by George Weiss, who had served as GM during the dynasty in the Bronx. Yogi Berra managed the Mets to the 1973 World Series, after nine years earlier guiding the Yankees to an American League pennant (it wasn't enough to save his job; he was fired after a loss to the Cardinals in Game 7 of the World Series). Willie Randolph played for two World Series–winning teams on the Yankees and served as a coach on four others. And Mel Stottlemyre was an All-Star pitcher for the Yankees in the 1960s and '70s before arriving as the Mets pitching coach under Davey Johnson, presiding over the staff that led the team to a 1986 World Series title. Stottlemyre returned to the Yankees as Joe Torre's pitching coach and was part of four additional World Series winning teams.

Now the Mets had sights on Kevin Long, who had spent the previous eight years as Yankees hitting coach, a stretch that included a World Series title in 2009. Long had multiple job offers, but saw the Mets as a franchise on the rise.

"I felt like they were ready to go, they were World Series capable," Long said in 2020, only months after the Nationals won the World Series with him as the hitting coach. "The Mets had a chance because of their pitching more than anything, and I know the value of good pitching. When you have those kind of arms, Harvey, deGrom, Syndergaard…it gives you a really good chance. I liked their team. I liked the organization."

Bolstering the team's interest in Long was his tight working relationship with Granderson, who struggled in his debut year with the Mets after four solid seasons across town. With Long back as his mentor with the Mets, Granderson's OPS rose from .714 the previous year to .821.

"I really clicked with Curtis in a lot of ways," Long said. "We enjoy each other's company, not only working in the cages, but hanging out. I love his parents. The number of times I have gone out to dinner with him and his parents, it's a lot.

"As soon as we got back together we started clicking again, and that's just the way it is sometimes. I tried with certain guys and they go somewhere else and they do better with another hitting coach. But for the better part of my career I have been the guy who has had the bigger impact, but sometimes it doesn't work out. In this case with Granderson it was two guys that get along and are really compatible."

CHAPTER 5

"NO"-HAN SANTANA

On the morning of June 1, 2012, the web site NoNoHitters.com, created by a Mets fan named Dirk Lammers, had updated to reflect the ridiculous truth for a franchise so built on starting pitching over 51 seasons.

The number 8,019 screamed across the page, denoting the games played by the Mets since their inception in 1962 without a no-hitter. The franchise of Tom Seaver, Jerry Koosman, and Dwight Gooden had 35 one-hitters, including five by the Hall of Famer Seaver. Among them was the heartbreak of Seaver's "imperfect game" on July 9, 1969, when Jimmy Qualls singled to left-center at Shea Stadium after the Mets ace had retired 25 straight batters, bringing his perfecto within two outs of completion. The Miracle Mets won the World Series that year, only exalting Seaver's masterpiece from that night against the Cubs.

For perspective, consider the Expos received a no-hitter only nine games into their existence in 1969. The crosstown Yankees had thrown five no-hitters (two of which were perfect games) in the Mets' lifetime. One of those no-hitters was thrown by none other than Gooden. There was also a perfect game by David Cone, whose brilliant career had blossomed with the Mets.

And Seaver, after he was infamously traded from the Mets to the Reds, threw a no-hitter on June 16, 1978, against the Cardinals. Also not forgotten are the record seven no-hitters Nolan Ryan threw after the Mets traded him.

Now, as a nondescript 2012 season was unfolding for the Mets, more than four years had passed since a serious no-hit flirtation had occurred. That dalliance belonged to John Maine, who took a no-hitter to the eighth inning at Shea Stadium on the penultimate day of the 2007 season. With two outs in the eighth, the Marlins' Paul Hoover dribbled a roller along the third-base line for the only hit allowed in what became a runaway Mets victory, but that was hardly the worst news of the weekend for the home team. The following day Tom Glavine got jumped by the

Marlins in the first inning, completing an epic meltdown in which the Mets squandered a seven-game division lead with 17 remaining.

This latest Mets season wasn't anything special, but at least Johan Santana had returned to reclaim his spot atop the rotation after missing the previous year rehabbing from surgery to repair a torn anterior capsule in his left shoulder. Santana was 33 years old and determined to show he could still be, if not an elite pitcher, an All-Star-caliber arm worthy of the contract the Mets had given him before the 2008 season. That deal ran for six years and was worth $137.5 million, a record at the time for a Mets player.

Santana had already proven his mettle to the Mets, even with the disappointment of his missed 2011 season lingering. The left-hander won two Cy Young awards with his original team, the Twins, but was embraced by New York fans as one of their own. Santana in return routinely professed his love of playing for the organization.

"I think the guy legitimately loved being a Met," said Bob Ojeda, who had joined Gooden, Ron Darling, and Sid Fernandez to form a dominant rotation that helped the Mets win their last World Series title in 1986. Ojeda was now serving as a studio analyst for SNY. "I don't think [Santana] was saying cliché bullshit like—I'll go back and just say it— Glavine. I mean, [Glavine] never loved the Mets. He'll lie to this day, probably, but that's a crock of shit. He was from Atlanta and it's like going to your nemesis and saying, 'Oh, I love it here, these guys are great.' It wasn't. He was doing what he was doing to get paid and keep pitching. But I think Santana legitimately loved being a Met, and he was a winner and he would have loved to do some postseason action here with the Mets.

"Santana didn't have any animosity when he got to the Mets. It was similar to me. I was in the American League and came over to the Mets. I was like, 'Who the hell is the Mets?' I didn't care, I got the uniform and then just bonded. And I think Santana just bonded with the Mets and Mets fans."

Johan Santana missed the 2011 season rehabbing from shoulder surgery, but returned strong the following year and took a shot at Mets history when he faced the Cardinals on June 1, 2012, at Citi Field.

Santana's third manager with the Mets, Terry Collins, came to appreciate the left-hander before he had even thrown a pitch for him. At the time, Collins had just arrived to the organization as the minor league field coordinator, in the final season of manager Jerry Manuel's tenure in 2010. One day in spring training Collins was left in charge of overseeing the workouts at the Mets' spring training complex as much of the team departed for a road Grapefruit League game. Collins was entrusted with monitoring the pitchers who had remained behind.

"They are going through these drills and half-speed kind of stuff," Collins said. "And all of a sudden Santana stops the drill himself and says: 'If we're going to be out here, let's do it right.' And that is when he captured me. That is when I said, 'This guy can pitch for me, any time.'"

Santana's upbeat personality carried through the clubhouse, leaving teammates to respect him for more than his elite talent.

"I got here and the first game I ever played was behind him," said former outfielder Jeff Francoeur, who arrived to the Mets in 2009. "I get here and he's got one of the clubhouse boys carrying a jukebox around behind him playing Michael Jackson on repeat. The energy Johan brought was awesome. You have pitchers when they are pitching that day, you can't even talk to them. You can't even say 'hi.' With Johan you could go in there an hour before he pitched and have a full-fledged conversation with him. I always appreciated that about him."

If there was a performance that had come to define Santana's tenure with the Mets to that point, it occurred on September 27, 2008, with his team desperately needing a victory to remain alive in the postseason race. Santana took the ball on short rest and gutted out a three-hit shutout against the Marlins at Shea in which he threw 117 pitches. It was such outings the Mets had envisioned when they acquired Santana from the Twins the previous offseason for Carlos Gomez, Philip Humber, Kevin Mulvey, and Deolis Guerra.

Years later David Wright would rank Santana's performance against the Marlins as maybe the best by a Mets starting pitcher in the third baseman's 15-year career.

"I got lucky to play behind Matt Harvey during a couple of those years, Jake [deGrom] during some of his years, Pedro [Martinez], R.A. Dickey when he won the Cy Young award," Wright said. "But Santana's [performance] might have been the greatest—under the circumstances and pitching on short rest—one of the greatest games pitched I've ever been on defense to witness. He was magical that day. Had to win and went out and pitched a three-hit shutout."

The fact a banged-up Mets team remained in the postseason race until the final day of the regular season in 2008 was a testament to Santana, according to closer Billy Wagner, who had watched the team fall short of glory the previous two years largely because it lacked such a presence in the rotation.

"He was Clayton Kershaw," Wagner said. "It's max effort for nine innings. He was one of those rare guys, he wasn't going to be satisfied with going seven innings and giving up three runs. He was looking to go nine and give up none. He was that one you wanted having the ball."

Four years later, an overcast Friday night with rain in the forecast to begin June didn't have the same vibrancy as a must-win game to keep the season alive. Carlos Beltran, who had been dealt from the Mets to the Giants in July the previous year, was returning to Citi Field for his first game since the trade. Many of the pieces were still in place for the Cardinals from a team that had beaten the Rangers in Game 7 of the World Series the previous year. Beltran had been added to help cover for Albert Pujols' departure to the Angels during the offseason.

The Mets' starting lineup this night was indicative of the depths to which the franchise had sunk in the aftermath of Bernie Madoff's Ponzi scheme. The Mets slowly began shedding payroll, and by the start of 2012 stars such as Beltran, Jose Reyes, and Francisco Rodriguez had departed without suitable replacements signed or developed.

Omar Quintanilla, a quintessential Quadruple-A player, was the starting shortstop on this night. Josh Thole, a light-hitting catcher who would be dealt to the Blue Jays after the season with R.A. Dickey in the trade that yielded Noah Syndergaard, was behind the plate. Slow-footed Lucas Duda started in right field, as the Mets tried to figure out how to carry two first basemen (Ike Davis was the other). Kirk Nieuwenhuis, who would bounce between Triple-A and the Mets for the next few seasons, started in center field. Mike Baxter, who had been claimed off waivers the previous year, was in left field.

But for star power the Mets had the 29-year-old Wright, still in his prime, albeit not the player whose career was on a Hall of Fame trajectory before he fractured his back a year earlier. Or some might contend the turning point occurred in 2009, when Wright was beaned by the

Giants' Matt Cain and never seemed completely comfortable in the batter's box again, especially against offspeed breaking balls.

And, of course, there was Santana, who had shown signs the left shoulder was healed. He went to the mound on this night for his 11th start since the surgery. He was 2–2 with a 2.75 ERA, after five days earlier throwing a four-hit shutout against the Padres in which he needed only 96 pitches.

* * *

Mike Baxter grew up in the Whitestone section of Queens, a hardened Mets fan cognizant of the franchise's no-hitter drought. It was just an additional piece of ammunition Yankees fans—who watched David Wells and David Cone throw perfect games in successive years in the late 1990s—needed in taunting Baxter at school or around the neighborhood. Of course, the Yankees' four World Series titles in five years (including one by beating the Mets in 2000) was enough to damage Baxter's psyche as a young baseball fan.

Baxter went from Archbishop Molloy High School to attending Columbia and Vanderbilt, before getting selected by the Padres in the fourth round of the 2005 draft. He had a dream realized five years later by making his big league debut for the Padres, for whom he played nine games before returning to the minor leagues the following season.

On this night Baxter was the Mets left fielder for what would become the defining game of the 232 he played in the major leagues over six seasons. Claimed off waivers by the Mets in 2011 after the Padres had released him, Baxter was on his way to becoming a short-lived journeyman, finished as a player before his 31st birthday. And this night in Flushing may have accelerated that course more than he could have anticipated.

Early on, the clues were difficult to detect that Santana was on his way to something special. The fact Santana had walked David Freese and Yadier Molina in the second inning, extending his pitch count to 40 as he got the third out, certainly didn't scream *historic*. Then Santana needed only 21 pitches to get through the next two innings.

"It was the fourth or fifth inning and it was a strange one because he was walking guys and it wasn't the cleanest game," Baxter said. "Usually when there is a no-hitter or perfect game there is a rhythm to it where it feels different than any other night. That one you kind of looked up and, 'Alright, he hasn't given up a hit, that's weird.' There was a little bit of traffic on base, and there's a couple of walks here and there and deep counts and high pitch count. As the game progresses you could feel a buzz in the stadium kind of growing."

Beltran's swing in the sixth inning should have ended the drama, except one of the greatest missed calls in Mets history interceded: umpire Adrian Johnson ruled Beltran's line drive behind third base was foul, despite evidence to the contrary in the form of a ball mark on the foul line. In 2012, a format for challenging calls wasn't in place, but even if replay had existed the play would not have been reviewable as the rules are constituted because the ball hit in the infield.

"I got a good look at it, and it could have gone either way," Wright said years later, laughing. "That is one of the ones where you kind of hold your breath a little bit because it was hooking. And it hit [the ground] and it's tough to see, but that was close, very close."

In the SNY booth, Keith Hernandez was sure of what he saw on replay: "That ball was fair…in the course of a no-hitter there are two, three, maybe four plays that are made, well this was a call, and [the ball] was fair."

Beltran hit Santana's next pitch sharply to Wright for a groundball out. The buzz was alive again in Citi Field.

* * *

Yadier Molina had broken the Mets' hearts six years earlier with his go-ahead homer in the ninth inning of Game 7 of the National League Championship Series, across the parking lot where Shea Stadium once stood. Now the Cardinals catcher was ready to deliver another dagger, with Santana chasing history. The shot Molina hit to left field in the seventh inning on this June night is forever frozen in Baxter's mind.

"I know it's not a home run, that is the first thing, because it wasn't high enough," Baxter said. "You know the ball is going to stay in the park and I had a read on it and I felt like it was a play that I could make."

It was Santana's 102nd pitch of the night. Santana watched the play in left field transpire, walked a few steps from the mound and placed his hands on his hips as he gritted his teeth, clearly uncomfortable with the view. Baxter was laid out on the warning track after crashing into the fence, the ball still in his glove. Teammates began racing to left field to check on Baxter.

"I kind of stumbled after I caught it," said Baxter, who hit the fence full-tilt with his left shoulder, which connected to the arm on which he wore his glove. "That is where the whole play broke down. It was a fine play, but I don't think it was this elite play or crazy good play. Unfortunately for myself, I couldn't brace for the wall."

Baxter was removed from the game and would soon receive the diagnosis of a displaced collarbone, along with torn cartilage on the top two ribs on his right side.

"I hit the wall with my left shoulder and the injuries were on the right side of my sternum from the force," Baxter said. "It wasn't a left shoulder injury, it was more the chest because of the impact with the wall and the momentum takes you into it. That is where some of the stuff kind of got messed up. I knew right away something was wrong, it just took a while to figure out what it was. It was a rare, unique injury for baseball."

Baxter was helped to the trainers' room, where X-rays showed the displaced collarbone. He would later find out about the torn rib cartilage.

The SNY broadcast remained on as Baxter was examined by the medical staff. Baxter was still an interested observer in the game.

Santana would retire Matt Adams on a grounder to first and complete the inning at 107 pitches. The wondering game had already begun as to whether the left-hander would continue. Before the game, Collins had set Santana's max pitch count at 115, and here he was nearing the limit and scheduled to bat second in the bottom of the seventh in a game the Mets led 5–0.

When Santana didn't immediately appear in the on-deck circle there was at least brief suspense. Had Collins decided to pull the pitcher? An ovation arose as Santana emerged from the dugout with a bat. As it turned out, Santana was late getting to the on-deck circle because he had retreated to the trainer's room to check on Baxter.

* * *

Mike Vaccaro pulled into the press parking lot at Citi Field not long after Baxter went to the trainer's room. Vaccaro, the *New York Post* columnist, had a scheduled off night, but once Santana survived the fifth inning hitless, the ritual began. Vaccaro grabbed the car keys and began a drive to the ballpark that would take maybe 40 minutes from his home in Bergen County, New Jersey, if he didn't hit traffic.

A passionate baseball fan who had attended 1,000-plus games as a fan and reporter, Vaccaro had never witnessed in person the final out of a no-hitter or perfect game. So over the previous decade or so, Vaccaro would drive to Yankee Stadium, Shea Stadium, or Citi Field during no-hit alerts, only to be disappointed each time.

"I probably did it six or seven times," Vaccaro said. "I remember I made it to Yankee Stadium when CC Sabathia had a perfect game going and talked the guy in the garage into letting me park the car there."

But the brightest of those memories for Vaccaro was driving to Shea Stadium as Glavine was continuing a no-hit attempt against the Rockies on May 23, 2004. The treat was listening to WFAN's radio broadcast, with Gary Cohen and Howie Rose.

"The whole time I am driving in, these two guys, they are savants and every one-hitter and close call in Mets history, without looking it up they just mentioned it," Vaccaro said. "And if you care about Mets history it was fascinating to hear these guys extemporaneously have this conversation while Glavine is mowing through the Rockies."

Vaccaro arrived that Sunday afternoon just in time to hear Cohen say that somebody named Kit Pellow had broken up Glavine's no-hitter with two outs in the eighth inning. Vaccaro never even bothered leaving the car, and returned home.

This night was different. Vaccaro not only arrived at Citi Field with the no-hitter intact, but got to the press box with the dream still alive. On social media, the "Vac Watch" had begun as friends and readers wondered in which inning he might arrive, attempting to chase this potential piece of history.

"At that point it had become a little bit of a thing, and I actually caught a little bit of traffic, so I was getting worried," Vaccaro said. "It's very rare I hit traffic going to no-hitters, but I hit a little bit of Friday night traffic and I was able to check on Twitter and it's crazy—almost like kids tracking Santa Claus. People were checking and wondering where I was.

"It's funny, because unfortunately Mike Baxter getting hurt really helped me because there was a delay in the game for a while and that really let me make up some time and I got there for the start of the eighth inning. I didn't think I would get there at all, but I got there kind of early."

I could certainly relate to Vaccaro. As a young reporter for the *Connecticut Post*, I was watching on TV at home in Stamford, Connecticut, one Sunday afternoon in 1998—a day off from covering the Yankees or Mets for the newspaper—when Wells took a perfect game against the Twins into the middle innings. Within 40 minutes I had arrived at Yankee Stadium and managed to squeeze into maybe the last available parking spot in a corner lot.

But I was disappointed approaching the stadium, just after the seventh-inning stretch—fans were departing, leaving me to naturally believe Wells had surrendered a hit. I went inside anyway, and to my surprise the perfect game was intact. A better story might have been captured that day standing by the exit of the ballpark and interviewing fans leaving early, asking them if they realized what was happening in the game. I'm guessing many of the early departures had come for the Beanie Babies giveaway, all the rage at the time.

After watching Wells complete his perfecto in '98, I was present for the entire game the next year, when David Cone retired all 27 Expos batters he faced—with the author of the only World Series perfect game, Don Larsen, in the house for Yogi Berra day festivities.

I had covered more than 1,300 games since then, but hadn't witnessed another no-hitter as Santana was working his magic that night. Now it was beginning to feel more real.

For Vaccaro, the feelings ran even deeper.

He recalled the first game he ever attended—Cardinals-Mets on June 29, 1974, Old Timers' Day at Shea Stadium. Vaccaro's father liked both the Yankees and Mets (yes, it's possible to root for both), but young Mike took his allegiance based on that initial trip to the ballpark.

"I became a Mets fan," Vaccaro said.

But another significant event happened that day.

"My father pointed to the press box and explained what went on there and that was the day I realized what I wanted to do," Vaccaro said. "I was seven years old. I was fascinated by the idea of actually making a living writing about baseball."

Jon Matlack was a tough matchup for the Cardinals that day, allowing only one hit in a shutout victory. The opposing pitcher, John Curtis, singled in the third inning for the Cardinals' only hit.

"As we were walking out of the ballpark, my father said, 'Do you have any idea what you just watched, you almost saw a no-hitter in your first game,'" Vaccaro said. "And I remember telling him, 'I'll see one eventually.'"

Almost 38 years later, he was still waiting.

* * *

Stationed in SNY's Manhattan studio, where he was handling pre- and postgame analysis for the network that night, Bob Ojeda had flashbacks to his own dance with a no-hitter.

Ojeda was pitching for the Red Sox against the Yankees late in his rookie '81 season when he took a no-hit bid into the ninth inning. Rick Cerone delivered a pinch-hit double to end the dream.

"I was in Yankee Stadium, a Saturday day game, and my father happened to be watching at home in California and I didn't get it done," Ojeda said. "I gave it up in the ninth, but we still won the game, which was cool. I left a runner on second base and we were up 2–1 and Mark Clear shut them down like nobody's business. Clear was a really good guy, and I remember after the game he told me, 'You were going to get that win.' It would have been cool to get the no-hitter, but sometimes it's not in the cards."

Now, as he watched Santana's flirtation with history, Ojeda was struck by the number of change-ups on which the left-hander was relying. The change-up had been Santana's weapon of choice throughout his career, but to Ojeda it seemed there was possibly another reason for his reliance on the pitch that night.

As a left-hander who had battled his own share of arm soreness throughout his career, Ojeda came to depend on a change-up because it was the pitch that caused him the least amount of discomfort.

"If you go back and look at the number of change-ups Santana threw for outpitches, if I am throwing my pitch, my outpitch is the one that hurts the least because that is the one I can be most accurate with, and he threw a boatload of change-ups," Ojeda said. "That is good and bad. Good because you can get through it and bad because your arm is deteriorating. I remember the dilemma of whether or not they should let him keep going."

* * *

Most every heartstring in Citi Field was pulling for Santana, but the pitch count told a colder, harsher reality: the pitcher would need not only the luck of avoiding a bloop single in the final two innings, but relatively low-energy outs were now essential.

"I am in that weird place that Terry Collins is probably in," R.A. Dickey recalled years later, referring to the Mets manager. "He's thinking the Mets have never had a no-hitter in the history of their franchise and this cat, he's throwing a no-hitter and his pitch count is getting dangerously high. But he wouldn't be taken out. Johan would have fought him, I think, if they tried to take him out.

"It's just one of those things where you are hoping every pitch he threw was going to be popped in the air, like every first pitch to every hitter, especially when it got past the seventh inning."

Tyler Greene provided a favor by swinging at Santana's first pitch of the eighth inning, hitting a pop-up to shallow left that Kirk Nieuwenhuis grabbed, avoiding a collision with Omar Quintanilla. Five outs remaining.

Next was pinch-hitter Shane Robinson taking a called third strike. Four outs remaining.

Santana lost the strike zone against Rafael Furcal and walked the shortstop. The walk was Santana's fifth of the night, but he recovered to retire Beltran on a weak line drive to second base. Three outs remaining.

The ninth inning went quickly. Matt Holliday lined out to center field, bringing Santana within two outs of the mission. Allen Craig followed with a fly ball to left field that Nieuwenhuis grabbed, bringing another roar from the 27,069 fans in the ballpark awaiting history.

"Johan had the great sinking change-up and he got tired and his change-up really became more effective the last three innings," Hernandez said. "He got better in the eighth and better in the ninth because he couldn't throw it as hard and it really started biting and sinking, almost like a spitter or a greaseball, and it made him more effective, and he knew it, too, because he went to his change-up. He didn't throw it for a strike. It's almost like Bruce Sutter's split-finger, and that was a very effective pitch down the stretch for him."

At 9:48 PM, Santana uncoiled and threw a full-count change-up that David Freese swung and missed. It was pitch No. 134.

"He's done it!" Howie Rose screamed on WFAN radio. "Johan Santana has pitched a no-hitter, in the 8,020th game in the history of the New York Mets! They finally have a no-hitter and who better to do it than Johan Santana, and what a remarkable story."

In the SNY booth, Gary Cohen, a lifelong Mets fan like Rose, issued his own farewell to the no-hitter drought.

"It has happened!" Cohen said. "In their 51st season, Johan Santana has thrown the first no-hitter in New York Mets history!"

Cohen, who had spent 23 years in the broadcast booth for the team without as much as the Mets taking a no-hitter into the ninth inning, was at a loss to fully comprehend what he had just seen.

"It was almost an otherworldly experience, not only because of the history, but also the circumstances of that night," Cohen said. "I think it all kind of tied together. My feeling from watching the franchise almost from its inception and seeing a half-century of Mets pitchers fail to accomplish this feat was that it was never going to happen. That it simply was a mark of the franchise that they would have great pitchers who often would throw no-hitters before or after they arrived, but would never throw a no-hitter for the Mets.

"And until the last strike on that night I would have told you the same, that it was just not going to happen, that it was not destined to be, that it was a feature of this franchise's fate. That's how I entered it and how I observed it until the last strike to David Freese. That was just part of the franchise's DNA."

But Vaccaro, who had raced to Citi Field to catch those final few outs, was a believer from the moment he arrived.

"I got there for the eighth inning and I saw those three outs and it's funny: sitting in the press box there, I honestly believed he would do it," Vaccaro said. "You want to write about cool stuff. I didn't grow up a Giants fan, but I loved the fact I was able to write about two Giants Super Bowls. I wasn't a Yankees fan, but I have written all of the Yankees' championships since 1996.

"So, yeah, I had all this Mets history inside me because I grew up a Mets fan, but just to be there for a real cool, historic moment, that's why I kept doing that. And for whatever reason I never doubted that Santana was going to get it done. I don't know why that is. Especially when it comes to the Mets, you always default to what's the worst thing that could happen?"

After Cohen wrapped up the SNY broadcast he headed to the radio booth, where he and his old friend Rose could reunite and digest what had just occurred. The duo chatted for 45 minutes on-air, putting a cap on the historic night.

Hernandez, who had largely remained in the background for the final innings of the SNY broadcast—he deferred to Ron Darling because of his partner's pitching expertise—remembers the surprise of seeing Cohen misty-eyed after Santana had completed the masterpiece.

"It shows what kind of fan Gary is, a Mets fan," Hernandez said. "He was teary-eyed, and I was stunned that he was in tears. Not sobbing, but emotional."

* * *

In the postgame delirium, Justin Turner (who was injured and didn't play in the game) went running into the tunnel leading to the clubhouse and delivered a present to Santana as he conducted an on-field TV interview.

Suddenly, Santana's face was covered with whipped cream.

"People were mad because I ruined the Mets' first-ever no-hitter interview," Turner recalled years later while playing for the Dodgers.

Before the media was allowed into the clubhouse for postgame interviews, Santana gave an impromptu speech to his teammates.

"Tonight we all made history, that's all that matters," Santana said. "It's thanks to you guys, because you guys make it happen. I was just doing my job, having fun."

Santana could barely contain his jubilation in the interview room.

"We worked very hard—all the things we have gone through that I have been through," Santana said. "This is very special and I know it means a lot to New York."

When it was finished, Wright, who would hardly describe himself as a memorabilia collector, decided he needed something to commemorate the night. Wright surveyed the dugout and found his bounty: the bat Santana had used during the game.

"I got him to sign it to me," Wright said. "I wanted a ball or something, and then I saw the bat he used in the game and I grabbed it."

Wright had previously never participated in a no-hitter at any level.

"Just the intensity was through the roof," Wright said. "And that was really cool to be a part of, especially since you can think of some of the

Mets greats that had an opportunity to throw a no-hitter and Johan is one of the best to put a uniform on. He had about as dominant a stretch as you could have in baseball and his first couple of years with us he was as good as anybody. I was real fortunate to have the opportunity to participate in his no-hitter."

The questions were just beginning for Collins, who became emotional during his postgame press conference as he recounted the gut-wrenching decision to stick with Santana, who previously had never thrown more than 125 pitches in a game.

The 63-year-old Collins, a baseball lifer, had come of age in a bygone era in which pitch counts were more a novelty than an inhibitor. Back then there wouldn't have been much question whether Santana would have remained in the game. But baseball had evolved as such that even 120 pitches for a starter was now considered stretching it. This was 12 years after Al Leiter had thrown 142 pitches for the Mets in losing Game 5 of the World Series against the Yankees.

Now the Mets had Santana, only 11 starts into his comeback after significant shoulder surgery, and Collins was ultimately the man who had to make the call on allowing him to chase history.

"I'm excited for him, but if in five days his arm is bothering him I'm not going to feel very good," Collins said, choking back tears. "You just don't jeopardize the whole organization, this season, for one inning, so we'll have to see how it is."

In the SNY studio, Ojeda was already wondering if Santana had been extended too far in chasing history.

"I was happy for him, but I did have big concerns," Ojeda said. "I remember I used the phrase on the postgame, I said, 'That game is going to live in infamy.' And then I was wondering if I misspoke and was onto something or if that was my subconscious pitcher/pitching coach mentality kicking in, going 'That one is going to pay a price and we will always go back to that game.'

"You throw a thousand games, but sometimes there's just that one that pushes you over the edge. There is a particular pitch, a particular number of pitches that is just your breaking point and I still remember using the word 'infamy' and thinking, 'I don't know if that's the right word, it's a tough word, but I don't believe I was misspeaking. I think it was my subconscious going, 'I know what just happened.'"

A week later Santana returned to the mound and surrendered four home runs in a shellacking at Yankee Stadium. The results were hardly much better in his ensuing start in which he allowed four runs over five innings at Tampa Bay. But Santana rallied with three straight superb performances, against the Orioles, Cubs, and Dodgers, that seemed to quell any concerns. Included was a three-hit shutout over eight innings at Dodger Stadium to conclude the month.

"It's been good," Santana said, referring to the three starts to conclude June. "A couple of tough games, but the good thing is that I feel good and I'm still competing and at this point we're still working and feeling good."

It would be the last time anybody saw anything resembling the Johan Santana that Mets fans had come to love over the last five seasons. Santana got clobbered in his next three starts, against the Cubs, Braves, and Dodgers, all losses in which he allowed at least six runs and failed to pitch beyond the fifth inning. On July 21, Santana was placed on the disabled list with a sore right ankle he sustained when the Cubs' Reed Johnson stepped on him as the pitcher was covering first base.

The Mets' belief was Santana's ankle injury had prevented him from landing properly during his delivery, leading to shoulder fatigue. Santana returned in August, started two games for the Mets and was then shut down for the season with inflammation in his lower back. He was 3–7 with an 8.27 ERA since the no-hitter.

* * *

Santana returned to Port St. Lucie, Florida, the following spring as an important piece of the Mets' rotation, albeit one that was now over-shadowed by Matt Harvey, who had arrived from Triple-A Buffalo the previous July and demonstrated he could fulfill the big expectations cast upon him, after joining the organization as a first-round pick from the University of North Carolina in 2010.

But if the Mets were going to compete in 2013, they needed a healthy Santana, especially after trading National League Cy Young award win-ner R.A. Dickey to the Blue Jays the previous offseason.

As the exhibition games began, Santana was still limited to play-ing catch, leading general manager Sandy Alderson to express disap-pointment the pitcher hadn't arrived at camp ready to resume from the mound. Clearly upset with Alderson's message to the media, Santana took to a bullpen mound and began throwing, ahead of schedule. Santana then avoided the media for a week, hoping he wouldn't inflame the situation.

"When I started working out, everything was fine," Santana said, noting that he backed off his throwing weeks earlier because of concerns about inadequate arm speed. "Instead of pushing it we just wanted to build it up, so when it's time to do it again we feel better and not just start pushing."

Two weeks later, Santana's Mets career was finished, after an MRI exam revealed a re-tear of the anterior capsule in his left shoulder. Santana underwent a second surgery on the shoulder and never threw another pitch in the major leagues, aborting one comeback attempt after tearing his Achilles tendon in an extended spring training game for the Orioles in 2014. He returned to spring training a year later with the Blue Jays, but never got on the mound.

In later years, Collins still had conflicted emotions over letting Santana chase the no-hitter given the manner in which the pitcher's career ended.

"With the knowledge I have, there probably isn't a correlation," Collins said in 2019. "But my gut tells me I don't know, but the [134 pitches] didn't help."

The fact Santana had a strong stretch to conclude June before going downhill in 2012 does little to placate Collins.

"When you are looking at the big picture, you are not even looking at the three weeks after the no-hitter," Collins said. "You are looking at the next two years, so that is where I was with the whole thing. It was gut-wrenching, but to have him come in and say, 'Hey, thanks,' that meant a lot.

"He deserved that chance. He had earned it through his career, he deserved it. This guy was one of the great pitchers of the game and he deserved that right to go out there and do it, and I respect my players."

In announcing Santana's second shoulder tear, Alderson exonerated his manager.

"I don't have any second thoughts over the way it was handled," Alderson said. "This is a back issue that was preceded by an ankle issue, neither of which pre-existed at the time of the no-hitter—this has not been a shoulder issue. So from that standpoint I don't see a direct correlation.

"As good an explanation as any is this is a substantial number of innings that have been pitched over the course of this season following a season of no activity other than rehab and this just might be…his body starting to complain."

Ojeda respects the fact Santana was willing to jeopardize his career to chase history.

"I remember thinking that he's got a big deal in his pocket, he didn't need the contract, so I thought it was a selfless thing to do," Ojeda said. "He had the mentality of, 'If this ruins my arm, I don't give a damn. I am not hurting my family and I am doing something this Mets organization has never had done in spite of the pitching history,' so I thought it spoke a lot of the type of guy he was."

Santana finished his career 139–78 with a 3.20 ERA and 51.7 WAR. As strong as those numbers were, he fell off the Hall of Fame ballot after only one year of eligibility for not obtaining the minimum five percent of the vote needed to remain in consideration.

"He was insanely good and a lot of guys said they even knew what pitch was coming," Wright said. "Not that day of the no-hitter, but in general they said he tipped his pitches quite a bit and they still couldn't hit it. It's just like a Bugs Bunny change-up, and he was dominant."

Santana wasn't the only player who might have wondered how June 1, 2012, changed his career: Mike Baxter was placed on the disabled list and didn't reappear for nearly two months. Baxter had a healthy .915 OPS in 65 at-bats for the season before the injury. When he returned, his production dipped severely. Baxter remained with the Mets through the next season before landing with the Dodgers and Cubs to finish his major league career in 2015. Maybe the numbers would have leveled off for him regardless of the injury, but Baxter also realizes he was in the best stretch of his career before hitting the left-field fence at Citi Field.

"It felt like right before I got hurt it was probably the first time in my career I was carving out a role," Baxter said. "Terry was giving me starts against right-handed pitching. It was one of the few times, maybe a six-week period, where I would show up to the ballpark and kind of expect to play and really felt that. It gave me a good boost of confidence and I really felt like I was making my way in the league."

Baxter gave it one last shot in 2016, but never advanced beyond Triple-A with the Mariners. He went to work for the Blue Jays in a front office capacity the following year before his alma mater, Vanderbilt, called with an offer to become the team's hitting coach and recruiting coordinator. In Baxter's second season at the school, Vanderbilt won the College World Series.

"When your playing career ends you get perspective," Baxter said. "You get to look back and look at a career through the lens of a

10-year-old kid in Queens or a senior in high school and you are like, 'Man, that is incredible.' In the moment, not that you take it for granted necessarily, but you are just a competitor, you are competing. You are trying to play at the highest level in the world.

"I was a bench player, a good pinch-hitter, and I carved out some time, and it wasn't necessarily a memorable career—obviously for me it was great—but it's nice to have a little footnote in Mets history. I do appreciate it. Those are my fondest memories: playing for the Mets over those three years, so I am very grateful for that opportunity the club gave me."

CHAPTER 6
OUT OF THE BLUE

Zack Wheeler couldn't believe what he was hearing.

The Mets right-hander spent the 2015 season rehabbing from Tommy John surgery, and still believed he had a bright future in the organization, even after general manager Sandy Alderson nearly traded him two months earlier.

Now, as the Mets were preparing to face the Dodgers in the National League Division Series, Wheeler presented to team brass what seemed like a reasonable request: he wanted to share the experience with his teammates.

"I asked to come up to New York, and the Mets wouldn't let me," Wheeler said. "I just wanted to be part of the playoff experience, even if it was in the clubhouse or in the dugout, just so I could be a part of the experience so when I came back I wouldn't be shell-shocked if I went out there for my first playoff game. I would already be used to the noise, the reaction, that type of stuff."

Disappointed the Mets rebuffed his request, Wheeler was about to receive another jolt.

"And then I was like, 'Can I get some tickets and sit in the stands even?'" Wheeler said. "They were like, 'You have to buy your own.' I wasn't going to buy tickets to watch my own team play, so I ended up sitting at home."

Wheeler eventually got over the snub and spent the next four seasons with the Mets before leaving for the riches of a five-year contract with the Phillies worth $118 million. But the snub also became a source of motivation for the pitcher, who ultimately never received the opportunity to pitch in the postseason for the club. Wheeler would spend all of 2016—which ended for the Mets with a loss to the Giants in the NL wild-card round—continuing his rehab from the surgery before pitching for three straight teams that missed the playoffs.

In the early evening of July 29, 2015 you would have had a difficult time convincing Wheeler he would still be around in two months to get snubbed by the Mets for postseason tickets, never mind that he still had 77 games to pitch for the team.

* * *

It was no secret heading into the July 31 trade deadline that the Mets coveted a right-handed bat to help boost an anemic lineup that was responsible for the team hovering just above the .500 mark.

Simply, the Mets were an ugly team offensively.

"I remember there was one game the Dodgers came in with Clayton Kershaw and I looked up and we had four guys that were hitting under .200 in our lineup," Noah Syndergaard recalled years later. "And Kershaw threw the easiest complete game three-hit shutout I have seen."

Justin Upton, Yoenis Cespedes, and Carlos Gomez were three of the prominent targets who emerged, with the Mets ready to jump on a deal. Gomez had started his career with the Mets, but was traded to the Twins in the deal that netted Johan Santana before the 2008 season. Gomez had since become an All-Star player with the Brewers.

"Gomez was certainly not as good a hitter and at the time slightly on the decline, but the spot that was a true offensive weakness for us was center field with Juan Lagares injured and declining," said Adam Fisher, then the Mets director of baseball operations under Sandy Alderson. "You are essentially replacing Lagares with someone who is almost as good defensively and is a pretty good hitter. That was the thought process. We all felt that we were overpaying for Gomez, but Sandy was being aggressive and it was just a really good fit and we were going for it."

In "overpaying" for Gomez, the Mets were prepared to send Wheeler and infielder Wilmer Flores to the Brewers. Wheeler had undergone his surgery four months earlier after tearing the ulnar collateral ligament in his right elbow in spring training. At the time he still hadn't blossomed into the pitcher the Mets thought they were receiving when they shipped Carlos Beltran to the Giants at the trade deadline in 2011. Flores was the lesser of the two players the Mets planned to trade for Gomez. A 23-year-old who lacked the agility to become an everyday player, Flores was shuffling between shortstop, second base, and third base for the Mets and producing at an adequate level offensively, primarily as a threat against left-handed pitching.

Reports of the trade began to surface on social media as the Mets were facing the Padres on July 29 at Citi Field. Flores was the starting shortstop that night for the Mets and Wheeler was in Port St. Lucie, Florida, watching the game on TV after a day of rehab.

"I was in the dugout when Flores came in and heard about the trade and you are trying to console him and he's still got to go out there and play," outfielder Michael Cuddyer said. "It was just weird. That was a weird day. There were a bunch of different media outlets going on at the same time with it, but us, the only way we were able to hear was in the clubhouse, where the game is on TV, and they are reporting it and yet he's got to out there every half inning and play on defense.

"And then he doesn't get pulled out of the game, so you know something hasn't officially happened, because especially in this day and age, the moment it even breathes, boom, you're out of the game."

The confusion carried into the eighth inning, when SNY's cameras caught Flores crying at shortstop. Manager Terry Collins, who to that point had been steadfast with Flores that he hadn't been traded, then had no choice but to remove him from the game.

Collins had first been alerted of the situation by injured David Wright, who was in the clubhouse watching on television. Collins pointed to the phone in the dugout that served as a direct line to the general manager's booth.

"And if Wilmer Flores has been traded, that phone is going to be ringing, because they are not going to let us play that guy, and it has not rung," Collins told Wright.

The manager pulled Flores aside in the runway leading to the clubhouse and told him to ignore the chatter and remain composed. But Flores, who had signed with the organization as a 16-year-old in Venezuela and dreaded the idea of leaving, wasn't about to be consoled.

"Well, the next inning he goes out there and he keeps crying," Collins said. "Now the phone is ringing and it's Sandy saying, 'You have got to get him out of this game. This guy is crying on the field.' I got him out of there, but that was pretty strange and when the game was over and we got to the bottom of the stairs in the clubhouse, Sandy was there and said he had not been traded."

Wheeler, watching in Florida, had seen the reports on Twitter before the chaos erupted involving Flores.

"I kind of already knew about it before Flores did, but I was sitting by myself and just chilling, watching the game and everything unfold on the field and all that," Wheeler said. "I was like, 'Flo, I feel you man,' because I was right there with him, so that was pretty wild."

Only adding to the confusion, Gomez tweeted about the trade, lending credence to the idea it was complete. But Alderson, concerned with Gomez's medicals—specifically a hip issue—nixed the trade with Milwaukee. That part of the story wasn't told until the GM addressed the media outside the clubhouse following the game. Flores was assured he would remain with the Mets and suddenly had endeared himself to a fan base moved by his show of emotion on the field.

In retrospect, Alderson says Flores probably should have been absent from the starting lineup with a trade imminent.

"We had no reason to believe the deal wouldn't go through at some point, but also there was no reason to play short at that time for a good portion of the game," Alderson said. "That is why I didn't inform Terry. I probably didn't anticipate social media and what might come out of either the Milwaukee camp or the player himself on the other end. It was an odd set of circumstances.

"I think that is the only player transaction in which I was involved with the Mets that was overturned for medical reasons. I should have anticipated [the story leaking]. But it led to great theater, frankly, so from that standpoint I don't regret it."

Among the developing conspiracy theories was that Mets owner Fred Wilpon had seen Flores crying on TV and told Alderson to kill the deal, using Gomez's medicals as an excuse. Alderson years later denied any conspiracy.

"But I am glad somebody told us to kill the trade—it happened to be a doctor—because what happened subsequently made a lot more sense," Alderson said.

Fisher was more blunt when asked about the theory Wilpon intervened.

"There is no fucking conspiracy," Fisher said.

* * *

Flores and Wheeler were still Mets, but the team still had a sizeable hole in the middle of the lineup and needed to pivot quickly. Contact was re-established with the Reds about the possibility of veteran slugger Jay Bruce, with Wheeler again serving as trade bait. But another name was resurfacing: Cespedes, the Cuban defector who had wowed fans in winning the 2013 Home Run Derby at Citi Field. Upton was also still a possibility.

Only adding to the sense of urgency to complete a deal, the Mets lost 8–7 to the Padres on July 30. The game was halted by rain with two outs in the ninth inning and the Mets ahead by two runs. After play resumed, Jeurys Familia allowed two base runners before Justin Upton smashed a go-ahead homer. The Mets had led 7–1 only two innings earlier. Now they were handed a loss.

"Ironically, I think the reason Upton was taken off the table by the Padres was because of that shocking loss on the Thursday afternoon, which I think gave [the Padres] some false sense of hope they could compete over the last two months of the season," Alderson said. "I think that is the reason they pulled Upton off the table. At some point it was ultimately Cespedes or nothing."

Cespedes was with the Tigers, his third team in two seasons, but the Mets were willing to ignore concerns about his makeup for a chance to add his powerful right-handed bat.

"There were two things with Cespedes why he wasn't at the top of the list going into the deadline," Fisher said. "First was the position fit. He only played left field at that point in the major leagues. He had an issue with the Red Sox when they tried to put him in right. We really didn't have a spot for him, we were going to create a spot for him. And then the cherry on top is he was a dynamic hitter, but he didn't have our approach, so you are talking about a twofold kind of negative where he really wasn't on the top of our list, not because of his ability, but because of the fit."

As July 31 arrived, Mets officials were trying to convince the Tigers to accept a trade that wouldn't involve right-hander Michael Fulmer, the organization's top pitching prospect now that Syndergaard and Steven Matz had arrived to the major league club.

But the Tigers stuck to their demand of Fulmer, a supplemental first-round pick in the 2011 draft. The Mets had received the pick as compensation from the Yankees, who signed veteran reliever Pedro Feliciano the previous offseason.

"There weren't a lot of people who wanted Cespedes," said J.P. Ricciardi, who oversaw the team's major league scouting. "It ultimately ended up being a group decision, but there were a few in the minority that wanted him and they were pretty adamant about trying to make the trade. Others didn't want to give up prospects. They didn't want to give up Fulmer, they didn't want to take a shot."

The previous four seasons of Alderson's regime had ended with losing records, without even a whiff of meaningful September baseball. And now the Mets were at a crossroads in 2015.

Already, Alderson had retooled the roster with trades that brought veterans Juan Uribe and Kelly Johnson, adding depth to the lineup and bench. Michael Conforto, the organization's top draft pick the previous year, had been called up from Double-A Binghamton to bring another bat. And the Mets fortified their bullpen by acquiring veteran reliever Tyler Clippard from the A's.

And then, with about 10 minutes remaining before the non-waiver trade deadline, the Mets went all in by landing Cespedes, surrendering Fulmer to the Tigers.

"That was our fifth year and for me personally, you don't get lifetimes to do these things," said Ricciardi, who had spent eight seasons as Blue Jays general manager without a playoff appearance before coming to the Mets. "You either step up to the plate and take your opportunity or sit there and let it pass you by. We could have passed and held on to prospects. It was ballsy, but it wasn't ballsy. For me, it was an easy trade to make."

In the lead-up to the deadline, Wheeler had called Alderson with a plea not to trade him. The pitcher had already survived a near-miss in the aborted deal with the Brewers and wanted the GM to know his heart was with the Mets. Once Alderson's focus shifted to Cespedes, the point was essentially moot, as the Tigers had become fixated on Fulmer. In the deal the Mets also surrendered minor-league pitcher Luis Cessa.

The following season Fulmer would become American League Rookie of the Year for the Tigers. Fulmer's performance dipped over the next 1½ seasons before he underwent Tommy John surgery in 2018.

"It's kind of what we expected—he had a huge injury file," Fisher said. "But we envisioned him as somebody who would be, since we had a pretty full rotation, an eighth inning–type guy who could give us coverage and potentially be a closer or mid-rotation starter. He was clearly our best pitching prospect at that point."

* * *

Cespedes arrived to a 53–50 team that was second in the NL East, behind the Nationals of Bryce Harper, Max Scherzer, and Stephen Strasburg. The Mets had their own studs in Matt Harvey, Jacob deGrom, and Syndergaard. Another piece to the rotation was 42-year-old Bartolo Colon, who continued to frustrate opponents with an 88-mph cutter. The bullpen had Familia, who had developed into a top closer after Jenrry Mejia was suspended 80 games early in the season following a positive test for Stanozolol, a banned performance enhancing drug. Mejia later failed two other drug tests and became the first player permanently banned from MLB for PEDs. He was granted reinstatement by Commissioner Rob Manfred in 2018, but the Mets released Mejia after two minor league appearances.

The lineup wasn't as blessed as the pitching staff. Curtis Granderson was a solid free-agent pickup before the 2014 season, signing a reasonable four-year deal worth $60 million. The team's captain, Wright, hadn't played since April after receiving a diagnosis of spinal stenosis, a likely byproduct of the stress fracture he had sustained in his lower back four years earlier. Wright was in so much discomfort in 2015 there were days he struggled to get out of bed. His only remedy was rest and physical therapy, leaving the Mets to wonder if and when he might play again.

Daniel Murphy was a defensively challenged second baseman who brought a dependable bat to the lineup and Lucas Duda added raw power to the equation. But much of the summer had been spent with names such as light-hitting Eric Campbell, John Mayberry Jr., and Kevin Plawecki in the lineup. It didn't help that the team's big free-agent acquisition from the previous offseason, Cuddyer, was banged-up for much of the season and clearly on the decline.

"I think we had to reinvent ourselves," Cuddyer said. "We were kind of floundering. Obviously our pitching was what kept us going up to that point. By no means or stretch of the imagination could we say our offense kept us afloat, but I just remember continuing to tell our pitching staff, 'Keep us in games. Keep plugging away and don't get discouraged.'"

Hours after the Cespedes trade was announced, the Mets were in a 1–1 game with the Nationals in the 12th inning at Citi Field when Flores walked to the plate against Felipe Rivero and homered into the left-field seats.

"Two nights ago he thought he was traded, in tears on the field, he gets his fourth standing ovation of the night as he ends it with a long ball," Gary Cohen said on SNY.

Cespedes was in the starting lineup the following night for his Mets debut and went hitless in three at-bats, but two homers from Duda led a 3–2 victory over the Nationals. A three-game sweep was complete the following night, when Syndergaard allowed only two runs over eight innings and struck out nine. Suddenly, these were the first-place Mets.

The roll continued with a three-game sweep in Miami and victory on August 7 at Tampa Bay that extended the Mets' winning streak to seven and gave them a 2½-game lead on the Nationals. Uribe contributed to the final victory in that stretch with a game-tying homer in the seventh inning.

The veteran third baseman, who had already belonged to World Series–winning teams with the White Sox and Giants, wasn't shy about showing off his championship rings as motivation for teammates. In later weeks, Uribe would become a spokesman of sorts for America's pastime, bemoaning the showing of college football and NFL games in the Mets clubhouse.

"More football, oh shit, fucking bullshit," Uribe trumpeted one Sunday afternoon in Atlanta. "Un-fucking-believable. Baseball, that is what I want to watch."

Uribe's distaste for football—or "foo-ball" as he pronounced it—became a running joke among the beat reporters covering the team. The following year Uribe signed with the Indians, and the Mets had a trip to Cleveland. In a media scrum before the first game of the series I jokingly asked Uribe what he thought of the Browns' chances for the upcoming season.

Unaware he was being trolled, Uribe responded: "Oh, I don't pay too much attention to football."

Cuddyer, though struggling at the plate, was another veteran who brought needed leadership to the clubhouse, especially with Wright sidelined. Early in the season, Cuddyer shared the idea of a "victory belt" that would be presented to the Mets player of the game following a win. He had started something similar with the Twins in 2008, giving out a ball to the player of the game following a victory. Then it became a game beer. Cuddyer brought the tradition to the Rockies, changing the reward. It changed again with the Mets.

"You find the personality of your team and back then everybody was talking about how much they loved the WWE," Cuddyer said, referring to the pro wrestling circuit. "It wasn't my thing, but I knew everybody enjoyed it. So [Kevin] Plawecki found a belt online and we ordered the belt and we started giving that to the champion of the game and it pulled us together. Everybody was rooting for one another. Nobody cared that they won the belt, they just wanted to see who it was that won the belt, and it was pretty special."

* * *

Cespedes brought the rawest power to the Mets lineup since Mike Piazza's prime years with the team or at the very least the early seasons of Carlos Beltran's tenure. The 29-year-old Cespedes had defected from Cuba four years earlier, escaping to the Dominican Republic, where he established residency. The fact he hadn't defected straight to the U.S.

allowed him to avoid the amateur draft and become a free agent, eligible for an instant windfall. The Athletics signed him to a four-year deal worth $36 million, the largest contract ever for a Cuban defector.

He was traded from the Athletics to the Red Sox and then to the Tigers and Mets, perhaps too much movement for a player with his skill set. So the Mets knew Cespedes would potentially bring drama to the clubhouse.

Terry Collins admitted years later that Cespedes was tough to keep happy.

"But you know what, so was Barry Bonds and he won four MVPs," said Collins, a former bullpen coach with the Pirates in the 1990s. "I knew at 7:05 I wanted to see his name in the lineup, I could tell you that."

Wright, the team captain, forged a bond with Cespedes early on.

"Some of the stuff with Cespedes is obviously self-inflicted, but genuinely he is a very quiet, mild-mannered, genuinely good person to be around," Wright said. "I think oftentimes people see his chains or the swagger that he has, the backward cap and they think he is this loud, boisterous outgoing guy that always speaks his mind and I would say he is the opposite. He is to himself, he is quiet. From what I have seen, at least the way he has always treated me, very respectful. I enjoyed it, other than some of the cigarette smoke."

Cespedes' first homer with the Mets didn't come until his 11th game with the team, on August 12 against the Rockies at Citi Field. But then he homered again two days later against the Pirates, and the Cespedes show was off and running. He would conclude the month with eight homers for his new team, which included a three-blast barrage at Coors Field in Denver on August 21 that ignited a seven-game winning streak for the Mets.

In the middle of that road trip, the Mets received another bat: Wright was cleared to rejoin the team after missing nearly four months rehabbing his back. The captain returned to the lineup on August 24 in Philadelphia and promptly homered on the third pitch of his first at-bat.

"I had to be careful, I almost pulled a Wilmer Flores out there," Wright said. "You try to keep your emotions in check."

The knockout punch in the NL East came during a trip to Washington in early September with the Mets already ahead by four games. The Mets blasted eight homers in the three-game sweep, leaving the Nationals battered.

Another key piece for the Mets had arrived just over a week earlier, when Addison Reed was acquired from the Diamondbacks just before the September 1 deadline to add players for potential postseason eligibility. In Jeurys Familia, Tyler Clippard, and Reed, the Mets had three right-handed relievers they could trust.

In totality, the additions of Cespedes, Uribe, Johnson, Clippard, and Reed over a five-week stretch had reinvented the roster.

"I think that really turned a frown upside down and at that point I think we really fed off the impact, because it was an understanding the front office is saying, 'We're going for it,' and we rode that horse as long as we could," Syndergaard said.

On September 24 they arrived in Cincinnati leading the NL East by 6½ games. The Mets won 12–5, reducing their magic number to one. With 60 cases of champagne hidden in a special storage area at Great American Ball Park, the Mets clinched the following day, receiving a three-run homer from Wright as the final dagger in a 10–2 victory. The Mets were headed to the playoffs for the first time since 2006.

"When I was laying on my back rehabbing for a few months this summer, this is what you dream of," Wright said. "This is what motivates you. This is what pushes you. This is what drives you."

* * *

Drama is the last thing anybody could have expected on a workout day at Citi Field three days before the start of the National League Division Series in Los Angeles, but Matt Harvey's absence was creating a buzz. His whereabouts were unknown.

The right-hander had returned from Tommy John surgery to perform at a high level for the Mets in 2015, going 13–8 with a 2.71 ERA, but created a stir in the previous month when his agent, Scott Boras, suggested Harvey was getting pushed too hard in his first season back and might benefit from an innings cap. Three years earlier, Stephen Strasburg (another Boras client) was shut down by the Nationals for the postseason because of workload concerns in his return from Tommy John surgery.

Harvey was 26 years old and had visions of a nine-figure contract, and wasn't immediately sure how to proceed.

"You understand the guy has got a whole career to look at in front of him, but as a veteran player not knowing how many times you are going to get back to the playoffs, you're just like, 'Damn, dude, we need you,'" Cuddyer said. "But I'm not so narrow-minded to not get the situation, as well.

"There were conversations, whether it was at dinner, but I never gave advice. I let him talk and let him get stuff off of his chest, because in my experiences that is best. Nobody really wants to hear your opinion. They just want to say their thoughts out loud, so they can hear their thoughts going on and then ultimately they have to make their own decision what they feel is best."

Initially, Harvey had failed to commit publicly to pitching beyond 180 innings. But from the Mets' perspective, shutting him down wasn't an option.

"We weren't going to shut him down, because the medical advice we were getting didn't warrant that," Alderson said. "That didn't mean that

Matt himself might not shut himself down or his agent might, but Matt is a competitor. If he could pitch he was going to pitch, and I think we all appreciated that.

"There was just no scientific evidence that 'X' number of innings was most appropriate and anything over 'Y' was a danger zone. There really wasn't any evidence to support that."

Now Harvey was missing from a noon workout a day before the Mets would charter to Southern California for their first playoff series in nine years. It was just the kind of story ripe to carry the back page of the New York tabloids. Where was Matt Harvey? Finally, he arrived at Citi Field near the end of the workout and apologized. Unclear was whether Harvey had overslept or gotten caught in traffic. One story presented to Collins was the pitcher had to drive his girlfriend home and lost track of time. Harvey had been spotted the previous night at a Tribeca steakhouse watching *Monday Night Football*.

"Obviously today was not the greatest," Harvey said, appearing in uniform in the press conference room after the workout had concluded. "I know we had a mandatory workout and the last thing I ever wanted to do is not be here with my team and basically there is no excuse, I screwed up and I wasn't there. I showed up a little late."

And then it was off to Hollywood for the Mets.

* * *

The Dodgers had two aces atop their rotation in Clayton Kershaw and Zack Greinke and were favorites to beat the Mets in the NLDS. The left-hander Kershaw had already won three Cy Young awards and would finish third in the results released after the World Series. If there was a crack in his resume it was his career 1–5 record in the postseason, which included meltdowns against the Cardinals in the previous two Octobers. The right-hander Greinke had completed the regular season 19–3 with a 1.66 ERA and would finish second behind Jake Arrieta for the Cy Young award, but it was Kershaw named as the Game 1 starter against Jacob deGrom.

Daniel Murphy homered in the fourth, and deGrom gave the Mets seven shutout innings in a 3–1 victory that served notice the underdogs had to be taken seriously. The intensity was about to increase. A night later, Chase Utley went hurtling into second base in an attempt to break up a seventh-inning double play and fractured the fibula in shortstop Ruben Tejada's right leg.

Utley had a long history with the Mets from his days in the NL East with the Phillies, but was also respected for his rugged, anything-to-win demeanor on the field. But on this night the Mets were convinced Utley had taken it too far: Utley was on top of the base when he had started his slide, prompting the creation of the "Utley Rule" the following season that disallowed such a tactic.

Adding to the Mets' discontent was the fact a replay challenge ruled Utley safe at second base, after Tejada's foot came off the bag. The Dodgers rallied for four runs in the inning and a 5–2 victory.

In the hallway leading to the visitor's clubhouse afterward, Alderson became incensed with MLB's vice president of operations Joe Torre over the Utley slide. Alderson still hadn't softened his stance years later.

"I don't think it was an appropriate slide and I don't think the umpires got it right," Alderson said. "I think they blew it. It's one of those things where you don't see it that often and then when it happens you get a little bit surprised by it and then you swallow your whistle, and I think that is what happened. I am glad the rule has been changed."

The series shifted to Citi Field, where Harvey would face Brett Anderson in the swing game. Collins, sensing the Mets would win—he was right, they rolled to a 13–7 victory—already had his eyes on Game 4, in which Dodgers manager Don Mattingly would have to decide between sending Kershaw back to the mound on short rest or perhaps using Alex Wood.

"The night before we are standing in the outfield, and I have known Clayton a long time because I was the farm director with the Dodgers when he signed," Collins said. "I asked him if he was pitching the next night. He said, 'They haven't told me anything yet.' And I looked at him and said, 'You're pitching tomorrow. You know it.' It was pretty funny. Then I got a message from him before the game, 'I'm pitching tomorrow night.'"

Kershaw dominated, allowing only a solo homer to Murphy in the fourth inning, leading a 3–1 victory for the Dodgers that sent the series back to Los Angeles for Game 5, in which deGrom would face Greinke. It was only fitting that such a tightly contested series should come down to two electric starting pitchers, even if deGrom at that point still hadn't become the elite performer who would win consecutive Cy Young awards.

On this night deGrom labored early. The Dodgers scored twice against him on four straight singles in the first inning. In the second, a walk to Joc Pederson and Wilmer Flores' throwing error put the right-hander in trouble. And then suddenly deGrom got it together, plowing through the Dodgers with ease. Nobody was a more interested observer than Syndergaard, who had been told before the game to be ready if deGrom got into trouble.

"I think I warmed up maybe four times during the game," Syndergaard said.

After that final warmup he was summoned to pitch the seventh inning. Murphy's home run, his third of the NLDS, had given the Mets a 3–2 lead against Greinke.

"When Murph hit that home run, I went, 'Holy shit,'" Collins said. "We got in a situation where I knew my best matchup in the game was going to be Noah Syndergaard, because I knew he was going to throw

105. That's what I remember is the end of that game and how those guys responded once we got the lead."

Syndergaard recorded three outs and Familia the final six, leaving the Mets within four victories of the franchise's first World Series appearance in 15 years.

* * *

The Cubs' journey to their first World Series title in 108 years was the kind of compelling drama that skyrocketed TV ratings, but a year before that 2016 magic they were overmatched in four NLCS games against the Mets.

More accurately, the series could have been called the Daniel Murphy show. The Mets second baseman had homered in the final two games of the NLDS against the Dodgers and then kept going right into the post-season record book. Murphy homered 14 times in the regular season and would halve that total in the NLDS and NLCS alone.

"Ultimately, if you look back on it Murphy went from a guy who tried to hit to all fields to a guy who tried to lift and drive and that made all the difference in his productivity," Alderson said. "He was an early example of launch angle and exit velocity, and you talk about 2015, launch angle wasn't really something measured all that much."

The previous year, the Mets chose Duda as their first baseman over Ike Davis based on Duda's exit velocity. Such a concept was a novelty at the time, but would become standard baseball operation within the next few years. Launch angle analysis was a step behind exit velocity.

"Another player we stuck with because of his exit velocities was Eric Campbell," Alderson said. "The problem with Campbell was his launch angles were like negative, but we really didn't know that at the time, but we could see that he didn't really lift the ball. It became pretty clear when launch angles began to be measured, and it's one of the reasons he wasn't as productive. But Murphy pretty much made himself into that kind of player and that is what he's been ever since."

Murphy's solo blast in the first inning of Game 1 against Jon Lester gave Harvey an early lead in the Mets' 4–2 victory. The next night Murphy hit a two-run blast against Arrieta in the first inning that gave Syndergaard fast support in a 4–1 victory.

"What sticks out the biggest was how cold it was in New York the first two nights, and our guys played like it was nothing," Collins said. "And you could actually see the Cubs were freezing. Arrieta wasn't the same, Lester wasn't the same, and of course our crowd energized us. The energy was electric and our guys were all fired up."

In Game 3, Murphy smashed a solo homer in the third inning against Kyle Hendricks and the Mets rallied against relievers Trevor Cahill and Travis Wood in a 5–2 victory. Allowing a run in the first, deGrom endured further shakiness early, but settled in to surrender only four hits over seven innings.

Duda's three-run homer in the first inning of Game 4 against Jason Hammel and Travis d'Arnaud's ensuing blast turned Wrigley Field into a morgue. Murphy unloaded in the eighth, giving him a homer in six straight postseason games, breaking the major league record set by Carlos Beltran in 2004 with Houston. The Mets won 8–3 to complete the NLCS sweep and were within four victories of the franchise's first World Series title since 1986.

It wasn't the last anybody would see of Kris Bryant, Anthony Rizzo, and Kyle Schwarber, who would be exorcising demons on the North Side of Chicago the following year, first by reaching the World Series and then by winning an epic Game 7 in Cleveland.

"Both us and the Cubs, neither team had been there before," Cuddyer said, referring to the 2015 NLCS. "So neither team was able to pull from their experience, and that NLCS helped the Cubs the next year, there is no question in my mind. But for us, I think the series prior, that Game

5, the way the L.A. series played out, gave us confidence we could go into the NLCS and do what we did."

* * *

J.P. Ricciardi is still angry at himself for Game 1 of the 2015 World Series. This is four years after the fact, with Ricciardi wondering why he didn't speak up louder when Collins unveiled his plan to start Cespedes in center field, leaving defensively superior Juan Lagares on the bench.

Cespedes had been a left fielder for the Tigers, but upon arriving to the Mets agreed to play center on a part-time basis, allowing Collins to use Michael Conforto and Curtis Granderson on the corners. Against lefties, Cespedes would shift to left field, putting Conforto on the bench.

But Cespedes was still raw as a center fielder, something Ricciardi had considered while watching the Mets work out at Kauffman Stadium before Game 1 of the World Series against the Royals.

"I'm looking at it from the front office perspective," Ricciardi said. "There are only so many times you can help your club. It's in the offseason, it's during the season with trades, and then in the postseason have as much information as you can have. I look back at that personally and I'm a little mad at myself on that one. Not that I was going to construct every lineup, but we could have had more information going to Terry and talking to Terry about starting Lagares."

The decision to start Cespedes in center backfired immediately; Alcides Escobar smashed Harvey's first pitch of the game to deep center, and Cespedes overran the ball. In a last-ditch effort for the catch he turned his glove for a possible backhand and ended up kicking the ball as he converged with the left fielder Conforto. The speedy Escobar raced 360 feet for an inside-the-park homer.

"Lagares makes that play in the first inning," Ricciardi said. "I know it's hindsight, but it wasn't hindsight, because the more I saw the outfield and the depth of it, and Cespedes not having enough experience playing center field, I knew. It's not Cespedes' fault we put him out there. That one bothers me, and we still had the game won."

The Mets had it won because Royals first baseman Eric Hosmer butchered a backhand on Wilmer Flores' grounder in the eighth inning, allowing Lagares to score the go-ahead run after he had singled and stole second. The Mets led 4–3, and their almost automatic closer Familia was returning to the mound for the ninth after recording the final out in the eighth.

Familia, utilizing a nasty sinker, recorded 43 saves in 48 chances in the regular season. In the postseason he was 5-for-5 and barely had been touched, allowing two hits in 9⅔ innings with six strikeouts and two walks.

But Alex Gordon was about to begin changing that narrative. On a 1-1 quick pitch from Familia with one out in the ninth, Gordon cleared the center-field fence to tie the game. The drama would last until the 14th inning, when Hosmer's sacrifice fly against Bartolo Colon brought in Escobar with the winning run.

"We spent a good part of the year telling Familia not to use the quick pitch—it wasn't effective, and that was true for a lot of guys," Alderson said. "And that ended up tying the game in the ninth inning and we ended up losing."

Adam Fisher, the Mets director of baseball operations who had helped formulate much of the scouting report on the Royals, took issue with the Escobar at-bat leading off the game against Harvey, but not because of who was playing center field.

Before the game, Fisher had given pitching coach Dan Warthen specific instructions: don't throw Escobar a first-pitch fastball. That message was supposed to be delivered to Harvey and the catcher d'Arnaud, but it may have gotten lost.

"I don't know why there was a fastball thrown to Alcides Escobar," Fisher said. "You are talking to somebody who was doing all the offensive advanced scouting. I don't understand why we threw him a fastball. I physically went to [Warthen] after the game and asked him, and all he could say was, 'I told them.'"

For the Mets there wasn't much to second-guess about Game 2. Though deGrom had pitched so brilliantly for the Mets in his first three starts of the postseason, he allowed a walk and five singles in the fifth inning to give the Royals a 4–1 lead. That was plenty for Johnny Cueto, who surrendered only two hits in the complete-game 7–1 victory.

The Mets were headed back to Citi Field in an 0–2 World Series hole, but there was at least one unaffected voice in the glum visitor's clubhouse at Kauffman Stadium.

"I still think we're going to win this thing," Warthen said.

* * *

The Royals had reached Game 7 of the World Series the previous year, losing to the Giants largely because they couldn't touch Madison Bumgarner. The experience may have hardened the Royals, a team built on bullpen and defense with a penchant for putting the ball in play.

Hosmer, Mike Moustakas, Ben Zobrist, and Lorenzo Cain were the important lineup pieces, and a bullpen that featured Wade Davis, Ryan Madson, Kelvin Herrera, and Luke Hochevar was as talented as any the Mets had faced that season.

"We're a small market team in Kansas City, the smallest of small, and you can't afford to go out and buy starting pitchers," said Dave Eiland, who served as Royals pitching coach from 2012 to '17 before joining the Mets in the same capacity. "So we built the pitching staff from the back end of the bullpen to the front. It's a credit to [general manager] Dayton Moore and his front office and the vision they had to do it that way. All our starters had to do was get us through five innings and we felt pretty good about things."

Wilmer Flores shed tears on the field upon hearing the Mets had traded him in 2015. The trade to Milwaukee was never completed, and Flores emerged as a fan favorite.

After winning 95 games in the regular season, the Royals survived the Astros in the ALDS and then beat the Blue Jays in six games to win the pennant. Taking a long view of the postseason when it began, Eiland liked the Royals' chances of winning the World Series.

"I told [manager] Ned Yost, Dayton Moore, and my wife when the playoffs started that if we beat Houston in the first round we were going to win the whole thing because there was nobody else in the playoffs that could beat us," Eiland said. "And I knew nobody in the National League could beat us. Toronto was going to be tough in their ballpark—I knew we would beat them in ours, which they turned out to be.

"Once we played the Mets I knew we could expose their hitters because they were all one-dimensional hitters. I was a little concerned about their pitchers shutting us down, but the offense we had, we didn't try to do too much. We just put the ball in play and used our athleticism. We exposed their defense, on the base paths and challenging their arms in the outfield."

The Mets would have to win two of three games at Citi Field to bring the series back to Kansas City. If the Mets still had a chance in the series it was because Noah Syndergaard, Steven Matz, and Harvey were aligned for the weekend. Certainly they could win two of three and apply pressure on the Royals, who were aiming to win their first World Series since 1985.

In Syndergaard, the Mets had the right man for the job in Game 3. The tone would be set on the first pitch of the game, when the right-hander fired a high-and-tight fastball that knocked Escobar off the plate. The pitch was premeditated to say the least.

"It was maybe after Game 1 that I started formulating it in my head, because I knew the previous series [against Toronto] and even before that he was swinging at the first pitch every time," Syndergaard said years later. "I was aware of that the whole time and I decided to just go with it. I was a naïve rookie that was kind of reckless at the time. Thinking about that moment still gives me goosebumps. I wouldn't change a thing if I were to go back to it."

In the opposing dugout, Eiland expressed taciturn approval.

"I remember it very well," Eiland said. "And when it happened the first thought that came to my mind was: 'It's about time somebody did that, because Escobar was [jumping on the first pitch] to every pitcher on every team for months.' I couldn't believe people kept throwing him first-pitch strikes out over the plate. I tip my hat for Noah doing what he did. He set the tone that night."

Escobar struck out, but the Royals still scored a run in the inning. The rest of the night belonged to Syndergaard and the Mets lineup: Wright and Granderson each homered in the 9–3 victory.

Afterward, Syndergaard's brushback pitch received much of the attention. And Syndergaard, sitting at the podium with his blond locks flowing from underneath a ski hat, wasn't amused when told Escobar thought the pitch was "stupid" because it had sailed so close to his head.

"I certainly wasn't trying to hit the guy," Syndergaard said. "I just didn't want him getting too comfortable. If they have a problem with me throwing inside, they can meet me 60 feet, six inches away. I've got no problem with that."

The Mets' momentum in the series was short-lived. Despite two homers from Conforto the following night, the Royals rallied against Tyler Clippard and Familia in the eighth inning with help from Murphy's error. The Royals scored three runs in the inning and won 5–3, giving Familia his second blown save in the series.

Now it all rested on Harvey to rescue the Mets and send the series back to Kansas City. The right-hander hadn't been anything special in Game 1, when he allowed three earned runs on five hits and two walks over six innings.

But on this night Harvey was sharp, accentuated by a fourth inning in which he struck out the side against the heart of the Royals' batting order—Cain, Hosmer, and Moustakas.

Granderson's homer in the first inning and a sacrifice fly from Duda in the sixth gave the Mets a 2–0 lead, which Harvey was entrusted with protecting. Once Harvey completed a perfect eighth inning, Collins was faced with a decision that would maybe define his legacy as Mets manager: give the ball to Familia or let Harvey, who was in the dugout lobbying to continue, pitch the ninth?

"I know all the stuff today, all the numbers, third time through the lineup, there was absolutely no indication this guy was losing it," Collins said, referring to Harvey. "He was dominant so much and I believe in adrenaline and his adrenaline was running so high, I said, 'This is our best chance.'"

Harvey began the ninth by missing with a full-count slider to Cain, who promptly stole second. Hosmer then jumped on an 0-1 pitch and doubled in Cain. Harvey had asked to return for the ninth, and now the decision was on the verge of blowing up on the pitcher, manager, and team.

"I respected it, because of everything that led up to that moment," Cuddyer said of Harvey's plea to remain in the game. "Everything that got talked about: innings limits and whether you're going to pitch in the postseason and Strasburg a few years before that. Everything that led up to that moment, for him to want the ball in the last inning, especially with the way he was pitching...that is what you want from your ace."

Eiland, from the Royals dugout, could understand Harvey wanting to return to the mound for the ninth inning. But the Royals pitching coach thought Collins' decision was the wrong one.

"I was somewhat surprised," Eiland said. "Harvey had done his job and they were ahead 2–0 at the time and you had a fresh bullpen. But I was shocked—absolutely shocked—when a runner got on base he didn't come out of the game. I can almost see where you send [Harvey] out there, but as soon as anybody gets on base he's got to come out of the game."

Hosmer now stood at second base as the tying run, as Familia entered for a shot at redemption after finishing with blown saves in Games 1 and 4.

Familia got Moustakas on a grounder to first base, with Hosmer advancing to third, for the first out. The tying run was 90 feet away, with Salvador Perez at the plate. Familia threw a 1-0 sinker that jammed Perez, sending a one-hop squib toward David Wright. Hosmer froze momentarily. As Wright side-armed to first for the out, Hosmer broke for the plate, and Duda's throw never had chance, sailing wide of d'Arnaud. It was just the kind of pressure the Royals had wanted to exert on the Mets and especially Duda, whose suspect throwing had caught the attention of advance scouts.

Familia, through no fault of his own, was hit with his third blown save of the series. But this time he would retire Gordon, who hit a comebacker that Familia turned into the final out of the ninth.

"We made a bad play," Collins said. "Lucas had a chance to throw the guy out at the plate and made a bad throw, but that is baseball. And once again, once we got in that Kansas City bullpen, I said, 'Oh, shit.'"

And that sentiment resonated in the 12th inning as the Royals were scoring five runs against Addison Reed. The Mets were finished in a 7–2 defeat that left them numb.

In the days that would pass afterward, a sense of accomplishment set in amid the disappointment of finishing three victories short of the ultimate prize.

"We had the No. 21 payroll in baseball and went to the World Series," Ricciardi said, referring to the Mets' rank on Opening Day. "They have parades for these people that have the 25th or 30th payroll in baseball and people rave about them. Nobody even mentions our payroll was 21st in baseball that year and we took a team to the World Series, so I thought as an organization we did a real good job that year.

"There was a lot of things that came together and they happened fast, so it was a joint effort in a lot of ways, and I thought it was probably our shining moment as a front office in that we had a chance to strike and we did, and if we didn't we would have never gone to the World Series again."

Wheeler, meanwhile, got over the postseason snub that included a denied request to join his teammates in the clubhouse and the Mets telling him he would have to buy his own tickets if he wanted to attend the games.

"It made me a little mad at the time, but it also drove me a little bit to get back and try to get to the World Series myself," Wheeler said. "I wanted to be up here with the guys and sort of be a part of it. There is no hard feelings, but I used that as motivation also."

CHAPTER 7
TRYING TO KEEP
IT TOGETHER

Noah Syndergaard had a good idea he was going to tear his lat several weeks before it actually happened.

In an effort to bulk up before the 2017 season, the pitcher joined a gym near his home outside Dallas, spending roughly $3,000 a month to work out with a group of athletes under trained supervision. Syndergaard carried the nickname Thor, but arrived at spring training resembling the Incredible Hulk, hardly the ideal form for somebody repetitively throwing a baseball.

"At that point everybody was doing the same workout, which I think is stupid," Syndergaard said. "Everyone has different goals, different body types, and different needs."

Syndergaard learned the hard way. After arriving to Florida, he sought out personal trainer Eric Cressey and a soft tissue specialist to learn more about his body and how it should perform. Both studied Syndergaard and informed him he had become a high risk to tear his lat because of his offseason workouts.

With baseball workouts already underway in Port St. Lucie, time was of the essence.

"We tried to mediate the problem as much as possible, but at that point you can't do much," Syndergaard said. "My overhead mobility and the way my scapula worked with the rest of my body at that point was pretty much crashing down. They kind of predicted it. They weren't too surprised when the lat tear happened."

The fact Syndergaard was a high risk for the lat tear came as news to Terry Collins and Sandy Alderson when I informed them about it in 2019. Collins offered a dismissive laugh, while Alderson wondered if Syndergaard's version of events was revisionist history.

"Syndergaard had a hard time listening to other people, but that is the first I have heard of that," Alderson said.

In the days before Syndergaard's start in Washington on April 30, the pitcher was diagnosed with biceps tendonitis. Alderson suggested further evaluation with an MRI exam, but Syndergaard brushed aside the idea, insisting he was fine.

On a change-up to Bryce Harper in the second inning of his next start, Syndergaard grimaced and reached for his right side, having torn the lat, sending the Mets' season into a spiral from which they would never recover. Within days, Yoenis Cespedes was headed to the injured list with a quadriceps injury, depriving the Mets of two elite performers.

"I don't know if [the MRI] would have done anything or not for Syndergaard, but it would have been prudent on our part if it had happened and it didn't, and that was my fault, my responsibility," Alderson said. "I should have insisted on it, and didn't."

Syndergaard still bristles at the idea an MRI exam would have prevented his injury.

"That drives me insane," Syndergaard said. "The MRI wouldn't have made a difference, because the start that I threw and tore my lat, the first inning I was throwing 100 and 101. An MRI is not going to show anything if you go out there and are still able to throw that hard."

The Mets' chances of reaching a third straight postseason had narrowed and within weeks were effectively dead.

* * *

Coming off their surprising World Series appearance in 2015, the Mets had enough young or in-their-prime quality pieces to believe October baseball would become a regular occurrence. The first miscalculation came before the new year, when the Mets extended a qualifying offer to Daniel Murphy, only to watch their postseason hero leave for the rival Nationals on a three-year contract worth $37.5 million.

But Murphy's postseason for the Mets wasn't a fluke. Though still defensively challenged, he finished second in National League MVP voting for the Nationals in 2016, after hitting .347 with 25 homers.

"I told Murph himself it was mistake not to keep him," Alderson said years later. "He had such a good playoffs and then in the World Series was pretty much shut down—offensively, shaky defensively—and I think we kind of thought, 'Here's the old Murph re-emerging,' but he continued to hit for Washington."

Adam Fisher, the team's director of baseball operations under Alderson, said Murphy's personality also played into the decision to let him depart.

"Just the brutal defense and the way he plays the game, all the goofy mistakes and the 'rah, rah' stuff," Fisher said. "I think a lot of us were just, 'Eh, it's time to move on and get a second baseman and a little better defender. Murphy...clearly made adjustments, but that he would be the player he was in the postseason takes a real leap of faith, and that is what he turned into. Good for Daniel.

"Hindsight completely 20/20, you trade Lucas Duda and put Murphy at first base. That is a better fit and you still can get Neil Walker to play second. A few years of [Murphy] as your first baseman and you're looking real good and that alleviates most of the issues."

The Mets turned their focus toward Ben Zobrist, one of the first players to carry the "super-utility" label. Team officials had received a good look at Zobrist in the World Series, as he posted a respectable .781 OPS for the Royals in the five games.

Zobrist got deep enough into negotiations with the Mets that he toured the New York City suburbs looking for potential places to live. He ultimately accepted a four-year deal worth $56 million from the Cubs that kept him close to his Midwest roots.

"I don't know if we thought we were getting [Zobrist], but he was clearly our No. 1 target," Fisher said. "We liked him the same reason the Cubs did, and he helped the Cubs win the World Series by being the exact player that we wanted. We just wanted someone with versatility, leadership, and a really good approach. He beat us with the Royals and he was so good."

The Mets pivoted to a trade, acquiring Walker in a deal that sent Jonathon Niese to the Pirates. The left-hander Niese was maybe most remembered during his Mets tenure for receiving a nose job at the expense of Carlos Beltran, who one day told the pitcher, "Hey, we need to get you a new nose." Niese received a rhinoplasty after the season that helped him improve his breathing.

Murphy continued to torment his former team every chance he received. In 2016, he batted .413 with seven homers and 21 RBIs against the Mets. He finished behind only Kris Bryant in the MVP race in helping the Nationals win the NL East.

Clearly, Murphy had become a steal for the Nationals, and that wasn't lost on the Mets after the season, with a team official pointing out that if the second baseman had accepted the club's qualifying offer the previous year, he would be staring at a much larger contract in free agency—perhaps in the neighborhood of nine figures—than he had received from the Nationals.

"We both screwed up," the Mets official said.

* * *

The offseason that included the Murphy decision was anything but normal for the Mets. Shortly after their World Series appearance, Alderson revealed he had cancer and needed surgery. The diagnosis had come weeks earlier, but Alderson was told the surgery could wait until after the Mets finished the postseason.

A few days after the World Series concluded, Alderson fainted during a press conference at Citi Field. With the GM meetings set to begin in Boca Raton, Florida, assistant general manager John Ricco and special assistant J.P. Ricciardi oversaw the organization, as Alderson prepared for surgery in New York.

"The problem with the surgery in November was they couldn't do anything," said Alderson, who has declined to specify the type of cancer. "They decided during the course of the surgery that they couldn't really do what they had planned because it was too extensive, so they basically sewed me back up and told me I would have to undergo chemotherapy first."

That treatment occurred in December, leaving Alderson at home in New York as Ricco and Ricciardi led the Mets' delegation at the winter meetings in Nashville.

Amid the Mets' pennant-clinching celebration at Wrigley Field two months earlier, Jared Diamond of the *Wall Street Journal* snapped a photo of Alderson sitting alone in the grandstand, after the ballpark had mostly emptied, as players partied on the field. Alderson was alone with his thoughts, his health among them.

"I just kind of sat down and tried to take in the moment, watching everybody else enjoy the outcome," Alderson said. "I get as much pleasure out of seeing other people happy as participating directly. There were probably a lot of things going through my mind, one of which was my health, which was uncertain at the time to say the least."

Alderson's second surgery occurred the following May and was successful. The GM had earned a measure of respect from the New York media months earlier when, still in a weakened state from chemotherapy, he walked across Manhattan in a blizzard to present an award at the annual Baseball Writers' Association of America dinner.

Over the years, Alderson used the dinner as a forum for some of his best quips. The previous year, with the Mets facing a gaping hole at shortstop and exploring various trades and free agents, Alderson was asked to present an award to Cal Ripken Jr.

"This is a big night for Mets fans, who have been waiting all winter for me to introduce a shortstop," Alderson said.

And Alderson brought heat the next year, following his walk across town in the blizzard. Noting that invited guest Matt Harvey lived in

SoHo and was absent from the event, he wondered if the "Greenwich Village airport" had been closed for the day.

* * *

Another key component of the front office, Paul DePodesta, surprised the organization by announcing his resignation in January of 2016 to become the chief strategy officer for the Cleveland Browns.

DePodesta had played football at Harvard, and his love for the sport never diminished. His legacy with the Mets was Brandon Nimmo, Dominic Smith, and Michael Conforto, all of whom had been selected in the first round of the draft. Kevin Plawecki arrived as a supplemental first-round pick after Jose Reyes had departed through free agency.

"I think Paul brought a smart, kind of systematic approach to the draft," Fisher said. "He had specific ideas, specific strategy, and we definitely started using analytics a lot more in the draft. In hindsight we had some pretty successful drafts when Paul was overseeing it. Paul is a smart guy and was certainly an asset to the organization when he was there. I think we were all surprised when he left. We had just been at the winter meetings with him and we were surprised with the timing and abruptness of it, but I don't think anyone was surprised that he was deciding to move on."

The Mets took a risk in DePodesta's initial draft with the team, selecting Nimmo, an 18-year-old outfielder, with their first pick. Nimmo, a Cheyenne, Wyoming, native, came from a high school that didn't field a baseball team, pushing him to the AAU and American Legion circuits. It wasn't until after DePodesta had departed the organization that Nimmo's major league debut occurred, in 2016. Over the seasons that ensued, Nimmo developed into the kind of solid player that validated his selection with the Mets' top pick in 2011.

The same couldn't be said of shortstop Gavin Cecchini, whom the Mets selected in a loaded first round in 2012. Among the players the team bypassed to take Cecchini with the 12th pick were Corey Seager, who went to the Dodgers at No. 18, and Michael Wacha, whom the Cardinals selected at No. 19. Another notable major league player, Marcus Stroman, was selected by the Blue Jays at No. 22 in that draft. Stroman and Wacha eventually ended up with the Mets later in their careers.

In DePodesta's final three drafts, the Mets selected Smith and Conforto in the first round. The team's first round pick in 2015 was forfeited as compensation for signing Michael Cuddyer, after he had received a qualifying offer from the Rockies.

"[Cecchini] was a bad pick, but even with him, he looked like he had a chance," Fisher said. "He performed real well at Double-A and Triple-A and wasn't able to make the jump to the majors. Cecchini is the only real big miss. Dom Smith turned out fine and you have got Conforto, and Plawecki hasn't been great, but he's been a serviceable major leaguer. There was a lot of depth, a lot of numbers."

* * *

The Mets received an unanticipated gift heading into the 2016 season when Cuddyer announced his retirement rather than try to play through the final year of his contract. By retiring, the 36-year-old Cuddyer forfeited $10.5 million—hardly a small sum for the player or a franchise that was constricted financially and sometimes had to dumpster dive for free agents in the offseason. Cuddyer struck a deal in which he received a $2 million buyout from the Mets to cover the difference in a backloaded two-year contract he had received from the club.

Cuddyer concluded the previous season on the bench, after posting a disappointing .699 OPS as he battled injuries. After undergoing double core surgery following the World Series, he decided the time had come to retire.

"I just felt like where I was in my abilities, where I was with my body, I didn't feel like I was going to be able to contribute to the level that was needed on the field," Cuddyer said. "Obviously, I still knew I could be a leader in the clubhouse and bring that, but I didn't feel like that was enough to warrant me going out there and getting what they expected they were going to get when they signed me. I didn't feel like it was fair to anybody involved, really."

It's almost unheard of for a player to retire with money remaining on a contract, even for somebody in Cuddyer's financial bracket (he earned about $81 million over his career). But to Cuddyer, the dollars were of secondary concern.

"It was tough, but I was very fortunate to be able to play a number of years in the big leagues and make that decision with my heart and my head as opposed to my wallet," Cuddyer said. "I definitely took a lot of crap from a lot of players who were like, 'Why don't you just sit on the DL the whole time and go through the motions?' But that is not me. That is not fair to your employers and I just felt like it was the right thing to do."

Following his retirement, Cuddyer was named a special assistant with the Twins, joining Torii Hunter, LaTroy Hawkins, and Justin Morneau as former star players in that organization to carry such a title. The new role allowed Cuddyer to remain at home with his three young children in the Chesapeake Bay region, but to stay involved in the game.

"I watch video on younger guys in the minor leagues and maybe throw my opinions out there or talk to those guys about experiences going through slumps or whatever the case might be," Cuddyer said. "There's four of us and we've all found our little niche in this role of what we like to do.

"My niche, if it's to the players, I like talking about the life of going through baseball, navigating your career. I'm not into the mechanics and coaching side as much. I like talking to guys about how to deal with professional baseball and then on the front office side of things, clubhouse chemistry. Do I think a guy can fit in the clubhouse? Do I think he will mesh with the guys we already have in the clubhouse?"

* * *

If there was a highlighted non-divisional home series for the Mets in 2016, it was their three games against the Dodgers on Memorial Day weekend. The series would be the first meeting in New York between the clubs since their emotional NLDS the previous year in which Chase Utley's aggressive slide broke Ruben Tejada's leg.

The Mets hadn't attempted anything close to retaliation during the postseason, but Utley was still a topic in the clubhouse during spring training, particularly after Tejada was released by the club.

Months earlier, Alderson had a chance encounter while playing golf at a private club north of San Francisco to which he belonged, but seldom visited. Alderson was playing alone, and another single waved him ahead.

"When I got up to the single, it turned out to be Utley's father-in-law, who was also a member of the same club," Alderson said. "He and I played four or five holes together and we didn't say one thing about the play at second base. I didn't raise it and he didn't raise it. We danced around that topic."

Syndergaard wasn't involved in such dancing as the Memorial Day weekend series approached. The legend of "Thor" had been fortified the previous year with the pitch he threw behind Alcides Escobar to begin Game 3 of the World Series. In a strange twist, the Mets and Royals opened the following season against each other, marking the first time in major league history the previous year's World Series participants met on Opening Day.

Noah Syndergaard reported to spring training in 2017 knowing there was a good chance he would tear his right lat after bulking up over the winter. That nightmare was realized in Washington on April 30 of that season.

In the second game of that series in Kansas City, Syndergaard, his golden locks flowing, took the mound and was taunted by the tune "American Woman" blaring through the sound system at Kauffman Stadium.

"I am sure they were trying to shake my game, but it made me kind of chuckle, like they even had the PA guys doing this too?" Syndergaard said. "It was ridiculous."

Syndergaard struck out nine batters over six shutout innings, giving him the Mets' only two wins against the Royals in their seven meetings beginning the previous October.

Now he was back to face the Dodgers for the first time since his electrifying seventh inning of relief in Game 5 of the NLDS. Providing Utley with a dose of discomfort was a priority.

"First and foremost, Chase Utley, I love the way he played the game," Syndergaard said. "He played hard. I have heard nothing but great things about him as a teammate, and competition in that kind of [playoff] setting, you really don't have time to think about things. It's just a do or don't kind of moment. I don't think that slide was intentional whatsoever, it just kind of happens."

That didn't change the fact Syndergaard felt he had a duty to perform during this Saturday night nationally televised game against the Dodgers at Citi Field. In the third inning, Syndergaard threw a pitch behind Utley and was promptly ejected.

"I think if you watch the replay of it, Rene Rivera was catching me at the time and I was so anxious that I had an opportunity for some redemption that Rene called a change-up away, and I was so fixated on this next pitch that I didn't even think to shake him off at all," Syndergaard said.

The fireworks had just begun. Terry Collins, irate that Syndergaard had been ejected without as much as receiving a warning, came storming from the dugout. The audio of his outburst was captured by a MLB microphone and became a sensation two years later when it surfaced. The audio was never supposed to be released, leaving MLB and Collins, in particular, embarrassed.

From that point, May 28, 2016 became known as the "ass in the jackpot" game.

"Tommy, that's fucking bullshit," Collins screamed at crew chief Tom Hallion. "You've got to give us a shot."

Hallion then informed Collins that Syndergaard's pitch behind Utley was the Mets' shot.

"Terry, I'm telling you: our ass is in the jackpot now," Hallion said.

To which Collins responded: "You fucking motherfucker."

The exchange would elevate Collins' status two years later among fans who had become disenchanted with successor Mickey Callaway's relatively dispassionate approach to the job.

Collins would have preferred if the audio never surfaced.

"I have got grandkids and all of a sudden my granddaughter goes to school and somebody says, 'My dad was watching a video of your grandfather last night and he's a really mean, nasty guy, you should have heard what he said,'" Collins said. "What the hell? How about somebody calling me and saying they are real sorry this got out?"

* * *

The biggest shock wave of the season had been delivered weeks earlier. In the San Diego twilight, Bartolo Colon stepped to the plate and lofted a fly ball to left field that just kept carrying. The hefty, nonchalant Colon had become a cult hero of sorts in his three seasons pitching for the Mets, and if this ball cleared the fence at Petco Park, the legend would add another layer.

Colon had arrived before the 2014 season to add a blend of experience and durability to a rotation that featured Zack Wheeler and would before long include Jacob deGrom. A year later, Matt Harvey returned from Tommy John surgery and Syndergaard and Steven Matz arrived from the minors, but the inability to keep all the young guns healthy simultaneously meant there was always a place in the rotation for Colon. It wasn't until April 2018 that the "Fab Five" of Harvey, Wheeler, deGrom, Syndergaard, and Matz took a turn in the same rotation together, and that party was short-lived: Harvey was traded to the Reds weeks later, breaking up the band.

Colon enhanced his mystique by conducting interviews in Spanish through an interpreter despite the fact he was comfortable holding a conversation in English. He previously served a suspension, after testing positive for a banned performance enhancing drug, but that became obscured by the time he joined the Mets. Simply, Colon was the "People's Choice" at Citi Field.

A rare glimpse into Colon's personal life was offered in 2016, when he was sued for child support by a woman who claimed Colon was the father of her two children. Colon at the time lived in New Jersey with his wife of 21 years and four sons. Taunted by fans at Nationals Park about having two families, the good-natured Colon managed to laugh off the matter. Colon told the antagonists he actually had three families.

On this night in San Diego, there wasn't enough "Big Sexy" to go around. He came to the plate in the third inning, delivered a level swing on James Shields' fastball, and, yes, it cleared the left-field fence for a home run.

"Bartolo has done it!" Gary Cohen screamed on SNY. "The impossible has happened…. This is one of the great moments in the history of baseball, Bartolo has gone deep."

The 42-year-old Colon had become the oldest player in major league history to hit his first career homer. Mets players hid in the runway connecting to the clubhouse, ensuring Colon—following a 30-second home run trot that evoked thoughts of grainy black and white footage of Babe Ruth circling the bases—returned to an empty dugout.

"Once I hit it, I knew it was gone," Colon said. "The ball in San Diego travels well."

The first clue such a moment was possible may have come in spring training, when reporters witnessed Colon clear the left field fence on a back field during batting practice. Teammates indicated they had seen Colon homer on several occasions during batting practice.

"We all had a hunch he was going to run into one, and it was going to go," Kevin Plawecki said.

Colon was selected to the National League All-Star team and finished the season 15–8 with a 3.43 ERA. After the season he was rewarded with a one-year contract from the Braves worth $12.5 million, but he struggled and was released by the team. He ultimately won another 12 games with the Twins and Rangers to surpass Juan Marichal as the winningest pitcher from the Dominican Republic. Colon took it a step further by winning his 247th game, to move ahead of Dennis Martinez for the most victories by a pitcher from Latin America.

* * *

Yoenis Cespedes' arrival at the trade deadline in 2015 helped carry the Mets to the World Series, but team officials thought of him as a rental, especially after his strong two months to conclude the regular season had increased his value on the free-agent market.

"We went into the offseason thinking he was going to get a monster deal that we weren't really comfortable with," Fisher said. "He had crushed it for us, but he didn't have a huge track record of being a superstar and didn't have our hitting approach and did not perform in the postseason, so we got to see some of the baggage close up, so we were comfortable with the approach we took."

That approach entailed the Mets waiting out the market on Cespedes. In late January the two sides agreed on a three-year contract worth $75 million that contained an opt-out after the first season.

"I don't think our hand was forced in any way," Fisher said. "We liked the player and when we were able to come to terms on something we felt like, almost a show me. Show me it's for real, that you can do it in New York for a whole year."

In addition to replacing Murphy at second base with Walker, the Mets signed veteran Asdrubal Cabrera to play shortstop, but third base became a black hole only two months into the season when David Wright's neck soreness became an issue, landing him on the disabled list.

The Mets' solution was a reunion with Jose Reyes, who had been released by the Rockies following a 52-game suspension for violating MLB's domestic violence policy. The previous offseason, Reyes was arrested in Maui for allegedly grabbing his wife by the throat and shoving her into a sliding glass door in their hotel room. The charges were later dropped after his wife decided not to cooperate with prosecutors.

Reyes' departure from the organization 4½ years earlier without the Mets as much making an offer was still a point of contention among fans who expected the shortstop to play his entire career with the club, alongside Wright. Only worsening the situation, the Mets had decided against trading Reyes the previous summer when perhaps they could have duplicated the Beltran-for-Wheeler deal.

Ricciardi years later said the Mets goofed in not trading Reyes.

"I think maybe in today's game we would have," Ricciardi said. "We probably shouldn't have put as much stock in the fans. I think sometimes we worry about what the fans think about the player and his tie to the organization as opposed to doing what's right for the organization, and I think we may have gotten caught up a little bit in that."

But Fisher offered a counterpoint to Ricciardi's argument.

"I have got no issues with the decision," Fisher said. "You think about what you can get and at the time we got the draft pick [which turned into Plawecki]. You are talking about a guy in Reyes who meant a lot to the franchise and we felt comfortable that the return, the draft pick return, was going to be comparable enough to what we would get in a trade that it made sense just to hold him.

"We also traded Beltran and there weren't a lot of teams jumping up and down for him. There wasn't much of a market for shortstops. We weren't being aggressive about marketing Reyes, but there also weren't teams banging down our door."

So Reyes remained with the Mets for the final two months in 2011 and became the first player in franchise history to win a batting title—he bunted for a single in the first inning of the season finale and was removed from the game with a .337 average, which was beyond the reach of runner up Ryan Braun.

Lured to South Beach on a six-year contract worth $106 million as the Marlins prepared to unveil a new ballpark, Reyes lasted only one season in Miami before owner Jeffrey Loria started dismantling the high-priced club he had assembled. Reyes was traded to the Blue Jays during the offseason, and later contended that Loria had told him only two days before the deal to buy a nice house in Miami. Reyes spent 2½ seasons with the Blue Jays before he was dealt to the Rockies in 2015 and openly complained about the state of the downtrodden franchise. That offseason he was arrested on the domestic assault charges. After signing a minor league contract with the Mets, a contrite Reyes promised to change his ways.

"I need to be a better man," Reyes said. "Be a better husband. Be a better dad for my girls. I got three girls, I need to be an example for them. I'm a human being. I made a terrible mistake. I say so sorry to everybody. I say sorry to my wife, my dad, my mom, to everybody. They know I'm a better person than that."

On the field, the Mets had trouble keeping pace with the Nationals, who were invigorated by Murphy's addition and watched younger players such as Anthony Rendon and Trea Turner develop. The Nationals still had Max Scherzer and Stephen Strasburg atop their rotation, almost guaranteeing they would remain competitive.

The Mets' rotation took a hit midway through the season when an underperforming Harvey was diagnosed with thoracic outlet syndrome and placed on the disabled list. At the time he was 4–10 with a 4.86 ERA, miles removed from the pitcher who had begged to continue into the ninth inning in Game 5 of the World Series the previous season.

It would worsen for the Mets. By August, both Jacob deGrom and Steven Matz sustained injuries that would end their respective seasons, leaving a gaping hole in the Mets rotation. Even Jonathon Niese (who returned from the Pirates at the trade deadline) became injured, leaving the Mets scrambling again.

Salvation arrived in the form of Seth Lugo and Robert Gsellman, two pitchers who had performed decently for Triple-A Las Vegas, but were hardly on anybody's radar previously. With Lugo and Gsellman stabilizing the rotation, the Mets had a chance. A needed bat for the lineup arrived in Jay Bruce, acquired from the Reds on July 31. But it didn't take long for "Bruce" chants to become "boo," as the veteran slugger slumped badly after arriving to New York.

And then there was Cespedes, who spent nearly a month playing through quadriceps soreness. If Cespedes' absences from the lineup weren't enough, there was the attached controversy that came with Kevin Millar tweeting a picture from the golf course of himself and Cespedes, on the same day the outfielder's quad discomfort forced him to the disabled list.

"The golf is bad optics, let's just start there," Alderson said. "Our doctors have told us that probably had no impact on the injury, positive or negative, but let's face it, to play golf during the day and then go out injured in the evening, it's a bad visual."

But if Cespedes' golf obsession was bad from a public relations perspective, it didn't translate into concern within the clubhouse.

"We wanted him to play golf, because every time he played golf he would hit a home run," hitting coach Kevin Long said. "He's got a lot of explosiveness to his body and I think it tired him out just enough where it took him down to 75, 80 percent. For him, that was a real good thing because he's kind of stocky and built. He's put-together, and when he's full of energy he still swings max effort and I think it's too much. I think the golf and the number of swings he took on the golf course, it wore him out a little bit and was just perfect."

After the Mets' 6–5 loss in Detroit on August 6, an angry Alderson paced the hallway outside the manager's office. Bruce had been thrown out at the plate to end the game, after Collins decided against inserting speedier Brandon Nimmo as a pinch-runner at second base. Infuriating

Alderson further, Collins didn't call for a replay challenge on the final play, which appeared close at the plate to the naked eye.

Collins' explanation for the decision to keep the slow-footed Bruce (who had arrived to the team only a week earlier) in the game was one he probably wished he could take back.

"Jay Bruce might be faster than anyone on our team for all I know," Collins said. "I know he is a good base runner."

With rumors swirling that Collins might be fired, the Mets' season continued to further unravel. A second straight loss in San Francisco two weeks later pushed the Mets two games below .500 and 5½ lengths behind in the race for the NL's second wild card.

But then the Mets got healthier. Cespedes returned to the lineup and players such as Cabrera and Curtis Granderson began to produce, with a boost from call-up T.J. Rivera.

Syndergaard, Lugo, Gsellman, and Colon gave the Mets a formidable rotation foursome even with Harvey, deGrom, and Matz sidelined, and Jeurys Familia was on his way to saving a franchise-record 51 games.

In a wild game on September 22, the Mets used 27 players—the most in team history—in what became known as the Cabrera bat-flip game. After Reyes had homered in the ninth against the Phillies to force extra innings, the Mets fell behind in the 11th. Cabrera, the go-ahead run, launched a shot to right field that he knew was gone immediately. As he watched the ball soar, he thrust both arms into the air, sending the bat flying. The 9–8 victory kept the Mets tied with the Giants atop the NL wild-card standings.

In all, the Mets went 27–13 over the final five weeks and not only clinched the wild card, but were the top seed, ensuring a home game against the Giants for the right to face the Cubs in the NLDS.

"I was really proud of the start we had to the season and we battled back with some key people missing," Collins said. "We lost Murph and

David was hurt. Jose Reyes was playing third base. We have Rene Rivera behind the plate, so I was very proud of that team to get us to the playoffs."

Only once previously (1999–2000) had the Mets reached the postseason in consecutive years. In an era before the wild card, the Mets won the World Series in 1986 before losing the NL East to the Cardinals the following year and returning to the playoffs in '88. Had there been a wild-card round in '87, the Mets (with 92 victories) would have been the top seed.

As well as Lugo, Gsellman, and Colon had pitched down the stretch for the Mets, there was no doubt who would get the ball for the first wild-card game in Citi Field history; Syndergaard finished the season 14–9 with a 2.60 ERA and had earned the organization's trust the previous postseason. And yet, the most heralded starting pitcher in the wild-card game belonged to the Giants.

In Madison Bumgarner, the Giants had one of the top postseason horses of this generation. That status had been earned two years earlier, as Bumgarner was named MVP of the NLCS and World Series, after pitching a shutout against the Pirates in the wild-card game. In five World Series appearances, the left-hander was 4–0 with a 0.25 ERA.

The Mets' angst was compounded by Bumgarner posing a threat to left-handed bats such as Granderson, Bruce, and Lucas Duda (who was benched in favor of defensively superior James Loney).

Syndergaard and Bumgarner matched zeroes for seven innings before Addison Reed picked up in the eighth for the Mets and kept the game scoreless. Enter Familia, back in the spotlight after getting charged with three blown saves in the World Series the previous year.

Brandon Crawford's double leading off the ninth put the Mets in immediate peril. Angel Pagan struck out and Joe Panik walked before Conor Gillaspie smashed a line drive over the fence in right-center. The homer accounted for all the scoring in the Mets' 3–0 loss.

"I remember going seven innings with nine or 10 strikeouts and Granderson making a huge catch in center field, a ball well-struck by

Brandon Belt," Syndergaard said. "That's all I really chose to remember, because watching them score three runs on that home run, it felt like somebody ripped my jugular out, ripped my heart out."

* * *

The 2017 season would be Terry Collins' seventh as Mets manager, and as it began there was little reason to believe his job was in jeopardy. After all, the team had rallied to secure a wild-card berth the previous season, putting Collins on a short list, with Davey Johnson and Bobby Valentine, as managers who had twice taken the Mets to the postseason. Valentine and Collins were the only Mets managers to reach the postseason in consecutive years.

But the 2017 season began crumbling quickly, following the torn lat that essentially ended Syndergaard's season and the subsequent leg injuries that kept Cespedes sidelined. With the team reeling, the focus turned to Collins, in the final year of his contract.

The previous year, Collins had hinted he might retire upon the completion of that contract. At the time he was 67 years old (the oldest manager in the major leagues) and contemplating his own mortality after a health scare in Milwaukee, where he was hospitalized and remained there overnight, following a pregame episode in which he became briefly disoriented.

But the subsequent wild-card run seemed to reinvigorate Collins, and by the time he arrived at spring training all talk of retirement had dissipated.

Collins, who had spent much of his adult life riding buses in the minor leagues—first as a player and then coaching and managing—couldn't have been more of a contrast to Alderson, the U.S. Marine, Vietnam veteran, and Harvard Law School graduate. But those differences may have allowed the partnership to flourish enough to see Collins become the longest-tenured manager in Mets history.

"I think the most important thing was [Collins] represented a different personality, a different set of experiences and sort of a different persona from the rest of us," Alderson said, taking into account his top assistants when he arrived, Paul DePodesta and J.P. Ricciardi. "Myself, Paul, even J.P. to some extent, but certainly Paul and myself being a little more buttoned-down, a little more analytical and less emotional and less volatile, and I thought [Collins'] contrast would be important, and I think it was. I think it definitely worked as long as it did.

"I thought Terry connected with Mets fans and I think he connected with the players for the most part, and he did have a different point of view, but I have to say this: our relationship was really quite complementary. We never got into arguments, he was very—I don't want to say 'compliant,' because that's not the right word—but we talked things through and we agreed 95 percent of the time."

The perception was Collins had arrived as a caretaker who would be replaced once the Mets were good enough to compete for the postseason. But the rebuild took longer than anticipated, and Collins continued to satisfy his bosses enough to keep the job.

The manager seemed to build equity with the front office particularly in 2011 and '12, as the Mets were surprisingly competitive before the All-Star break both seasons.

"I think we hired the right guy," Ricciardi said. "In fairness to Terry, they weren't good clubs that we gave him. We had financial limitations, they were coming off the Madoff stuff and Sandy was really just trying to straighten the chairs on the Titanic a little bit.

"Terry was the right guy at the time because he wanted to manage again, he had experience, we knew it was going to be rough. Terry was a good soldier. He took the bullet. He knew there wasn't a lot of talent and knew there was going to be some struggles and he put up the good fight. I don't know if too many people could have done a better job with the talent we had at the time."

But with the success of a World Series appearance and subsequent wild-card berth, Collins was held to a new standard. The Mets were now expected to win, and the grumbling behind the scenes escalated as the team began a free fall in 2017.

Alderson publicly stood behind his manager, but privately there were questions about Collins' game decisions, most notably his handling of the pitching staff. On at least one occasion the manager had been told by the front office not to allow a starting pitcher to work through the batting order for the third time, but ignored the advice. And when the pitcher struggled in the middle innings, the blame fell on Collins.

With the Mets removed from the playoff race, Duda, Bruce, Granderson, Walker, and Reed were traded, leaving Collins with a skeleton roster, and by September it had become clear he wouldn't be asked to return as manager.

"Win or lose, I don't know how many years [Collins] had left in him," Kevin Long said. "It's a grind. Managing in the big leagues is not easy, and he did it real well for a long time and it probably just ran its course. It didn't help that we were losing and had a bunch of injuries and things just didn't go the way we planned. But at the end of the day he should have no regrets on what he did as the New York Mets manager."

Before the final game of the season in Philadelphia, the manager paced through the outfield with a phone pressed to his ear. After the game, he announced his resignation. Alderson later named Collins as a special assistant to the general manager.

"Cespedes, when he blew that quad out, if you think it's easy to replace one of the finest players in the game, it isn't," Collins said. "You are asking guys who are good players to produce, but they are not superstar players like this guy could be. When you miss a superstar player it's tough to fill that role. David [Wright] wasn't there and Cespedes wasn't there. Hey, look, our guys played as hard as they could play, it just wasn't good enough. We created a team that was supposed to win."

* * *

After seven years of relative stability with Alderson and Collins working together, a manager's search was underway. A fan favorite had been removed from the mix a year earlier, when Wally Backman was forced out as manager at Triple-A Las Vegas. The former Mets second baseman, known for his scrappy play with the 1986 World Series–winning team, had been a finalist for the managerial opening when Collins was hired before the 2011 season. The consolation prize for Backman was a job managing in the minor league system, where he oversaw players such as Syndergaard, Matt Harvey, Jacob deGrom, Brandon Nimmo, and Michael Conforto at various points.

Largely popular among players, Backman had become an irritant to a front office that valued player development over winning games in the Pacific Coast League.

Alderson had also become concerned that Backman was leaking information to the media, so much so that the GM stopped directly communicating with him. Any thoughts that Backman might be next in line to manage the Mets were crushed after the 2014 season, when Collins recommended adding him to the major league coaching staff, only to be rebuffed by the front office.

Five finalists emerged as Collins' potential replacement: Long, Joe McEwing, Manny Acta, Mark DeRosa, and Mickey Callaway. From the group, only Acta had previous big league managerial experience. Long was popular among Mets players and well-regarded by the front office after 11 seasons as a major league hitting coach.

"I was either going to get the job or I was going to move on," Long said. "At that point I felt like I could really help and be a solution there and if I wasn't going to be given the reigns, I didn't want to watch somebody else do it. When I went for my interview I was prepared, I was ready, and I did a heck of a job in there, but it wasn't obviously good enough."

Callaway, the Indians pitching coach, was the surprise choice for the job. Long interviewed for the Nationals' managerial opening—which went to Dave Martinez—and ultimately accepted the hitting coach position with Washington.

"I got two runner-ups, which doesn't do me a whole hell of a lot of good," Long said. "But I am grateful for the experience, and at that point I was real gung ho on managing and once I didn't get it, I kind of backed off. I really like my job as a hitting coach and really like what I do."

As part of their shake-up, the Mets also fired Dan Warthen, who had served as the team's pitching coach for 9½ seasons. The quirky Warthen had become popular with Mets pitchers, especially the young starters he had helped nurture since their arrival to the big leagues. But it was Warthen's human side that appealed to the Mets pitchers as much as anything.

LaTroy Hawkins, who had pitched for the Mets in 2013, recalled him and Warthen sharing a bond in that both had daughters who were only children.

"I was always asking how he would do it, being so far from home for so many months with a wife and daughter," Hawkins said. "He told me something that I took to heart: he said, 'I make sure I take her to school every morning when I am home. I make sure I cook her breakfast every morning.' I will never forget those conversations we had about our daughters and our wives and how to navigate it. Once I got to the same age with my daughter it just made it a little bit easier. I knew how to react to it because of Warthen."

CHAPTER 8
THE CAPTAIN

The official naming of David Wright as the fourth team captain in Mets history occurred at a hastily arranged press conference following a spring training game in March 2013.

Jonathon Niese was about to be named the team's Opening Day starter, bad news in the sense it meant ace Johan Santana wouldn't be ready to start the season (the left-hander was on the verge of finding out he had torn the anterior capsule in his shoulder for the second time and would undergo surgery), and the Mets needed a diversion.

Wright's ascent to captain was in the works for weeks, but announcing the honor on this day would serve as the perfect cover for Santana's setback that was sure to carry the back page of the New York tabloids.

A clearly agitated Terry Collins sat at the table in the press conference room at the Mets spring training complex. Briefly blinded by the stage lights, Collins blurted out, "I can't see shit" just at the moment SNY went live to his microphone for the announcement.

Wright joined Keith Hernandez, Gary Carter, and John Franco in the fraternity of Mets captains. Collins had lobbied for the designation for his third baseman after Wright agreed to a contract extension the previous December.

"One of the biggest things I ever did was when I went to Sandy [Alderson] and Jeff [Wilpon] and asked them to make David the captain," Collins said. "Because I thought his presence, the way he dealt with people, it wasn't about team meetings. But he would get somebody off to the side and say, 'Hey, you need to pick this up a little bit.'

"David is undoubtedly one of my favorite people I have ever been around because the way he is with people, his respect for the game, his respect for the guys who play the game and the way it is supposed to be played. His respect for the media…when David Wright was there he was always there and always ready to answer a question. He never belittled anybody, handled it professionally."

Wright had become the face of the franchise years earlier, as the talented homegrown boy with the good looks whom every father—at least among Mets fans—wanted his daughter to marry. Wright, even more so than Derek Jeter across town with the Yankees, largely managed to keep his personal life off the gossip pages.

The Mets had faced a monumental decision on Wright following the 2012 season. His contract ran for another year, but if that deal was allowed to expire he would almost certainly head to free agency and hunt for the highest bid on the market.

In a savvy move during general manager Omar Minaya's tenure, the Mets bought out Wright's arbitration years and signed him to a six-year deal worth $55 million. But to keep the All-Star third baseman in a Mets uniform for the remainder of his career, the cost would be much greater. Even so, Wright had made it clear from the start to the Wilpons and general manager Sandy Alderson that he would be willing to accept less to stay with the only organization he knew.

Alderson handled one facet of the negotiations in person, traveling to Wright's home in the Chesapeake Bay area and spending part of the day playing golf with the third baseman.

A year earlier, Alderson had let another homegrown star, Jose Reyes, depart through free agency. Not extending Wright's contract and watching him potentially escape through free agency had the makings of a public relations nightmare for the Mets, still mired in the fallout from Bernie Madoff's Ponzi scheme. The pressure was on Alderson to strike a deal that would prevent Wright from leaving.

"In that particular case, in addition to thinking David was a very good player—obviously with whatever risk is associated with a multi-year contract—it was also one of those branding issues, where we needed to do this for the reputation of the organization and the Mets brand," Alderson said. "One of the indirect benefits of signing David was David when he signed really strongly and publicly endorsed what we were doing, what our goals were and what the future held, and he publicly stressed how confident he was that we were headed in the right direction the next couple of years.

"I think there were some other things that kind of reinforced that feeling on the part of Mets fans, but I think that was really important, so that was an indirect benefit of the contract, but I don't think you can discount its importance."

The new contract was worth a franchise-record $138 million over eight years. Santana's deal with the team had been for $137.5 million, the same dollar figure Jacob deGrom received from the Mets when his contract was extended before the 2019 season.

At the winter meetings in Nashville, Tennessee, the Mets announced Wright's new deal. If Wright had waited another year and tested free agency the thought in the industry was he could have received a contract worth at least $200 million. The chances of the Mets extending that kind of offer were close to zero.

"I'm humbled, privileged, emotional," Wright said at his press conference. "It was very important for me from Day 1 that I finish what I started. Things haven't gone the way we would have liked the last couple of years, but that is going to change."

* * *

A rare wisp of controversy enshrouded Wright during spring training 2015, when he and reliever Bobby Parnell attempted to put rookie Noah Syndergaard in his place.

During an intrasquad scrimmage, Syndergaard returned to the clubhouse and started eating lunch. Wright approached Syndergaard and began explaining that he belonged in the dugout watching the game. To accentuate the point, Parnell, standing nearby, grabbed Syndergaard's plate and tossed it into a garbage can. The incident became a big story because it had occurred during a window in which the media had been allowed into the clubhouse to speak with participants who had already departed the game.

"When you are a veteran guy you certainly don't want to be a hostile environment by any stretch of the imagination," Wright said. "But I think it's good sometimes, in an animated way, to let players know—not necessarily black-white, right-wrong—but how we should expect to do things and how things in a perfect world should be done.

"Noah probably could have snapped me in half if he wanted to, but I hope he respected and saw it from my side. To this day I'm very apologetic: I didn't know the media was in there. But I think that was part of the role of being a captain, was sometimes there's some unpleasant conversations to be had, and as uncomfortable as it may be, sometimes it's for the best."

Wright had grown up in such a culture in the Mets clubhouse. Upon receiving the William J. Slocum award for long and meritorious service from the New York baseball writers at their annual dinner months after he had played his final major league game, Wright recounted an unpleasantry of his rookie season with the Mets: he had to wash John Franco's back in the shower. Franco, then the team captain, set the tone for the rest of the clubhouse.

In his first spring training, Wright recalled returning to the clubhouse ahead of the veterans, ecstatic that lunch meat would be served. On the minor league side, Wright had grown accustomed to a steady diet of peanut butter and jelly, so lunch meat might as well have been filet mignon.

"So I am loading up all this lunch meat on my sandwich and was one of the first ones in there to eat lunch," Wright said. "And the next thing I knew, every day after that Johnny would go in there and get the lunch meat tray and put it in my locker, just to prove a point that this 21-year-old kid is in there eating before the All-Star veteran types.

David Wright became the Mets' "Face of the Franchise" during a 15-year major league career that began in 2004. Elevated to team captain, he spent most of his last four seasons rehabbing from injuries, surgeries, and spinal stenosis.

"It was stuff like that where I learned not only to respect the game, but to respect the guys who had come before me in the game. It was nothing malicious at all and I got a huge kick out of it, but he taught me a lot of baseball lessons."

But times had changed dramatically by the time Syndergaard was arriving to the Mets in 2015. The older school mentality of Billy Wagner telling Lastings Milledge to "know your place, rook" barely applied, and within a few years would almost disappear completely from the Mets clubhouse and many others. Syndergaard put the line of demarcation in the Mets clubhouse at Matt Harvey's arrival to the big leagues in 2012.

"When Harvey got called up it was a constant reminder by veterans in the clubhouse, 'Yeah, you have got great talent, but you're a rookie, so sit down and shut up' kind of thing," Syndergaard said. "I feel like he might have been the last person of that era, that kind of mentality was on its way out."

Syndergaard watched Pete Alonso set a major league rookie record with 53 homers in 2019 and isn't sure if the first baseman would have produced such a grandiose total under the old unwritten rules that said first-year players should be seen and not heard. Alonso was among the most colorful players in the Mets clubhouse almost from his arrival, bringing a little boy's passion and enthusiasm to a room of professionals.

"It's tough to say how good a year Pete Alonso would have had if we didn't encourage him to be himself," Syndergaard said. "I feel like him acting like himself he was able to flourish. There was a little bit of that when I played with Harvey, but I can't imagine what it was like when he came up with LaTroy Hawkins and John Buck and those kind of guys. Those were as old-school as they get."

* * *

Wright grew up in an area that became something of a hotbed for baseball talent in the late 1990s and early 2000s. From the Chesapeake Bay region in Virginia, Ryan Zimmerman, Mark Reynolds, B.J. (Melvin) Upton, and Justin Upton were among the players who joined Wright in forging notable major league careers. But the godfather of the group was Michael Cuddyer, the ninth overall pick by the Twins in the 1997 draft.

A shortstop who became a third baseman, Cuddyer served as a role model for Wright, who was four years younger.

"That is who I wanted to be," Wright said. "I was at the middle school that fed into his high school and we shared a baseball field with his team, and just seeing him work and the effort he put in, at the time he was a bigger shortstop and I was a bigger shortstop. He was a guy being recruited by all the ACC schools where I wanted to go, and I wanted to be him. I visited Florida State because that is where he signed."

It was only natural that when Cuddyer hit free agency following the 2014 season, after an injury-abbreviated year with the Rockies, Wright began recruiting him. Once the Rockies extended a qualifying offer to Cuddyer—meaning the team that signed him would have to surrender a first-round draft pick—it was assumed the Mets would pass on Cuddyer, then a left fielder.

"[Wright] was the first person that called me when free agency started and the only person that still called me when I got the qualifying offer put on me," Cuddyer said. "He was the only person that called me back, so he was definitely instrumental in me coming over there."

The two friends were together for the Mets' run to the World Series in 2015, even if both weren't right physically. Wright had returned from spinal stenosis for the final five weeks of the regular season and the post-season and Cuddyer was relegated to backup status in the outfield following his own injuries that forced his retirement after the season.

But October 2015, frozen as a moment in time, will always hold a special place for the two friends.

"It was very cool for our community here in Chesapeake that I still live in and we'll talk to people and still listen to their stories about where they were watching the game and all of that," Cuddyer said. "I every once in a while look through my phone and the photos of us and the photos of that time and it brings a smile to my face. It was a great run. It was a great moment of my career. A great moment of our careers, our lives, and obviously with the way the last few years went after 2015, it's one of the highlights as well. For both of us it was a great climax to the careers."

* * *

Wright's major league debut came on July 21, 2004, against the Expos at Shea Stadium, a game in which he went 0-for-4. Among the veterans who immediately embraced him were Cliff Floyd and Joe McEwing, who wanted to ensure the highly regarded rookie was comfortable in his new surroundings.

"A good-looking kid coming up and immediately a fan favorite, but that means nothing if you aren't balling or ready for the opportunity," Floyd said. "When I took him under my wing it wasn't like a heavy wing where you are giving him the business every single day to make sure you mold him into something. It was more like telling him what he needed to do every day: 'Make time for yourself. Do not make time for the media, make time for yourself first, the media will respect that. Be accountable and be at your locker every day. When you mess up, hold yourself accountable…and then go out there and ball. If you do that, you will be fine in this city, because you already have everything you need to be an amazing ballplayer, barring any crazy injuries.'

"It started off fantastic, it couldn't be better. We kept it light, we laughed, the whole little corner we had over there was cracking jokes consistently and he could just go out there and be himself…. As far as understanding how amazing he was going to be, I knew that from what I saw."

Wright finished his first major league season with 14 homers and a .293 batting average in 69 games. The other piece of the infield's transformation, Jose Reyes, had arrived to the Mets during the 2003 season. The Mets hadn't received an injection of homegrown youth of that caliber in such a short time frame since Dwight Gooden and Darryl Strawberry's arrival in the 1980s. Whereas drugs and alcohol derailed those two possible Hall of Fame careers, injuries dampened Wright and Reyes' chances of reaching full potential.

Among Wright's qualities was a natural affinity with the media, transforming him into something of a team spokesman early in his career, even in a clubhouse loaded with veterans. By 2006 that cast included Floyd, Carlos Delgado, Carlos Beltran, Billy Wagner, Tom Glavine, and Pedro Martinez. But pitchers, who aren't involved every day, generally aren't approached by reporters in the clubhouse post-game and asked to provide comments about the team's play. And stars such as Delgado and Beltran didn't embrace the role—leading Wagner in a 2008 postgame rant to remind reporters, "They speak English, believe me." It left Wright as a magnet for anybody with a notebook or microphone.

"I remember feeling bad on a nightly basis for David, because he was the guy who would have to stand there and do everything," Glavine said. "A lot of that comes with David being who he was and what he meant to the team, but it's one thing for a guy—obviously he is going to have to talk about his own performance and the team to a certain extent, but you have to have other guys there doing the same thing. [Wright] wasn't the only authority on what was going on with the team, so when you kind of thrust everything on one guy's shoulders, it can get to be a pain for that one guy."

Floyd, who departed the Mets following the 2006 season, said it was Wright's upbringing and humility, added to his natural talent, that made him perfectly suited for New York. Wright had grown up the oldest of four sons to Rhon Wright, a police officer, and his wife, Elisa.

Raised in a household as one of four boys, all of whom were spaced three years apart, competition came naturally to Wright.

"It would always be me and the youngest versus the two middle brothers," Wright said. "Whether it was basketball or ping-pong or eating. We would get a pizza and it would be a race to see who could get the most pieces. Everything was always a competition. It certainly helped me out because it gave me that competitive [drive], even at a young age, like I want to win and we would do anything it took to win these stupid competitions we were having as kids.

"The first thing that jumps out was I was lucky that the competition, I learned it at a young age because the worst thing that could happen was letting the two middle Wright brothers win at anything."

It went without saying that Wright respected his parents' authority. And that came through to his teammates with the Mets.

"If your kid is going to respect their elders it generally means he's a humble kid that understands failure comes when you least expect it," Floyd said. "You are coming up and you think everything you do is going to be amazing. Everything you do you are going to succeed. How many people have you seen hit the wall who think they are going to be the best ever? A lot.

"It's because they don't understand that aspect of it. I really think [Wright] understood that coming up and he could weather any storm that was presented to him, and that in itself was something I immediately admired about him. It's, 'This kid gets it, he's different than just baseball. He understands things around the game that he shouldn't know, but he already understands and that's a credit to his parents and his upbringing.'"

* * *

Wright's career was on a Hall of Fame trajectory through five calendar years in the major leagues. To that point he had been selected to four straight National League All-Star teams and won two Gold Gloves. A turning point might have occurred on August 15, 2009, when the Giants' Matt Cain drilled him just above the brim of the helmet with a 94-mph fastball. Wright was diagnosed with a concussion and taken by ambulance to the Hospital for Special Surgery in Manhattan. Wright missed two weeks before returning to the lineup for the final month.

But the mental scar remained.

"Whenever there were breaking balls, he buckled," Jeff Francoeur said. "He never was the same on the breaking ball again."

Francoeur could relate—he was hit in the face in 2004 as a minor leaguer and underwent seven hours of surgery, during which two plates were inserted. High-and-tight pitches, he says, spooked him for the remainder of his career.

"I would say David's approach and his fearlessness at the plate might have changed a little," Francoeur said. "Until you walk in those shoes and understand what it feels like, it's not that easy."

Wright disagrees with the notion his beaning by Cain marked a career turning point.

"I had a couple of my better years after that, so I don't think that is true," Wright said. "But certainly if you go and get hit in the head it's not a good feeling, but I was lucky to get back in there in September and kind of hop back up there on that horse. To say it was easy would be a lie, and it was a challenging time for me, but it certainly didn't affect the rest of my career by any means."

Even before the beaning, Wright's home-run total had dissipated as he struggled in adapting to pitchers-friendly Citi Field, which had opened that year. Wright finished the season with only 10 homers after blasting 33 the previous year with Shea Stadium as his home ballpark.

Wright rebounded with 29 homers in 2010 and played in 157 games. But the following April he was involved in a play that likely had reverberations for the remainder of his career. Wright dived to tag the Astros' Carlos Lee and felt pain in his lower back. After playing through discomfort for nearly a month, Wright underwent an MRI exam that revealed a stress fracture in his lower back. He missed two months and struggled through the worst season of his career upon returning, finishing with a .771 OPS.

But Wright's 2012 season, in a newly configured Citi Field that more benefited the hitters, was strong enough to earn him the team-record contract extension. Wright hit .306 with 21 homers that season and finished sixth in the National League MVP voting.

Wright started the All-Star game at Citi Field the following year, but was limited to 112 games because of a late-season hamstring injury. In 2014 his production nosedived (he finished with a career-low eight homers in 134 games), and another injury—this time a rotator cuff inflammation in his left shoulder—ended his season in early September.

So when Wright went on the disabled list with a hamstring strain the following April, there was more concern about the captain's durability. It wasn't until a month later the Mets revealed Wright was battling spinal stenosis, a chronic condition in his back that limited his movement, and would require extensive rehab and physical therapy. Wright's return for the Mets' run to the World Series in 2015 perhaps created the illusion he was indestructible. So even when Wright underwent surgery for a herniated disk in his neck the following June, he was sure he would return.

"The biggest fear that I ever had was how my back felt in 2015," Wright said. "That was the most doubt that I ever had crept in my mind, because there were days I couldn't stand upright. It was too painful to stand upright. That's where I was like, 'Oh boy, this isn't good.' After I kind of got through—I won't say overcame it, because it's never going to go away—but after I kind of got through that and kind of slowly worked back, I had that thought I was invincible again. 'Yeah, my back stinks, I am going to have to stay on top of it every day, but I can do this.'"

But Wright aborted a comeback attempt late in the 2017 season to undergo shoulder surgery. A month later he underwent surgery to alleviate the pressure on his lower back. Just how much physical adversity could one man take?

"For me it was always, 'I can do it, I can do it, it's just another hurdle,'" Wright said. "It didn't really fully kick in and I didn't quite comprehend the physical problems I had until I tried my last rehab in 2018. That was when I fully understood I couldn't do it physically, but until then it was always this 'can-do attitude that I will overcome'—and I genuinely meant it or thought it, that I could overcome anything. That there was no surgery that could stop me from coming back and being an All-Star caliber everyday player."

* * *

Yoenis Cespedes cared enough to show up, but was mysteriously absent for the main event.

In a lost season under rookie manager Mickey Callaway, the Mets decided to give David Wright a proper sendoff. After 2½ years sidelined, Wright would start at third base for the Mets on September 29, 2018, and then call it a career.

Wright still had two years and $27 million remaining on his contract, but it had become obvious his body wasn't going to cooperate to fulfill that obligation. In August he had started a minor league rehab assignment, with plenty of off days built in, to prepare for the possibility he could be a September addition to the Mets' roster. Finally, it was decided he would be activated for the last series of the season, against the Marlins at Citi Field.

Cespedes, at home in Florida recovering from heel surgery, was invited by team COO Jeff Wilpon to attend Wright's farewell. Wilpon so much wanted his star outfielder there that his private jet was dispatched to pick up Cespedes and bring him to New York.

As the team was stretching before the game, Wilpon paraded Cespedes, still in his street clothes, onto the field.

"I think collectively the whole team just kind of rolled their eyes," an observer said.

Cespedes changed into a uniform and would watch from the dugout on this night. Wright, batting third, walked in his first plate appearance of the game. He then came to bat leading off the fourth for what was decided would be the final plate appearance of his career.

Somehow, Cespedes missed it.

The outfielder, known for his penchant to enjoy a jolt of nicotine, was in the indoor batting cage area smoking a cigarette as Wright came to the plate for the final time. Cespedes' absence didn't go unnoticed in the dugout, given the lengths Wilpon had gone to get him there.

On Trevor Richards' second pitch, Wright hit a pop-up that first baseman Peter O'Brien caught in foul territory to a chorus of boos. By the time Wright returned to the dugout, Cespedes had retreated from the batting cage area, in time to at least give the illusion he had seen the at-bat.

"I remember many a day going down to that cage between at-bats and feeling like I need a fan to blow out all the smoke down there," Wright said in 2020 after hearing the Cespedes story for the first time. "The fact that [Cespedes] took Jeff's plane, he made it, I got a chance to say hello to him, I got a chance to see him, the fact that he made it is enough for me."

Wright's final at-bat seemed all too familiar to Keith Hernandez, watching from the SNY booth. Hernandez, years later, recalled his own final plate appearance in a Mets uniform. It came on September 27, 1989, against the Phillies' Jeff Parrett at Shea Stadium.

"I was very observant of what Wright was going through," Hernandez said. "He hadn't played a lot, he couldn't have been sharp. I had been hurt a lot [in 1989] and wasn't sharp and just didn't want to strike out. I hit a lazy inside-out terrible swing flyball down the left field line, shallow, and David basically popped up on the opposite field on the first base line as a right-handed hitter so there was some similarities there. It brought back my moment and it was almost like we shared similar experiences."

Wright returned to play defense for the fifth inning, before he was removed to a standing ovation. His next stop was the television booth, where he appeared still in uniform. Hernandez teased Wright on the air, telling him he probably would have hit seventh on the Mets team that won the World Series in 1986.

Over the years Wright had come to accept such ribbing from Hernandez, a former team captain, comparing it to the varsity team giving the jayvees a hazing.

But the relationship had always remained cordial.

"As long as I'm hitting in front of Keith it would be fine," Wright later said, when reminded about Hernandez's jab that Wright would have hit seventh on the '86 Mets. "We can go down the road if he wants to, but he's great. He is one of those old-school baseball types that you could sit down and just listen, and to me that is really special."

As a TV analyst Hernandez has tried to maintain a distance between himself and the players, but took a liking to Wright.

"We had a very good relationship and I wish more of the players would be like him," Hernandez said. "But I'm not a guy that likes to impose on players. There's a lot of media in New York, but it's my job to go down there to the clubhouse and I am kind of reluctant to do that."

O'Brien returned to the visitor's clubhouse and found a ball on his chair autographed by Wright with the message, "Haha, you should have let it fall." As a gag, one of the clubhouse attendants had signed the ball and left it for O'Brien, who had doubts about the authenticity.

But the first baseman later had the idea to seek an autograph from Wright to commemorate the occasion. A clubhouse attendant took a fresh ball to the Mets clubhouse and had Wright sign it. Wright, showing the sense of humor that made him so popular as a teammate, inscribed, "No, really, you should have let it drop," on the ball and sent it back to O'Brien.

"I would have liked another chance to try to get a hit," Wright said. "But it wouldn't have felt right had he let it drop and then I got a hit."

For Wright, the night provided a sense of closure. He had received an opportunity—with his young daughters in attendance for the first time—to play third base for a few innings again and say goodbye to a fan base that largely adored him over 15 seasons.

In the regular season finale the following day he sat as a spectator on the bench and soaked in the sounds one last time.

"Certainly, physically, the Mets could have said 'You can't play,' which was 100 percent the truth, but it was very important to me and I pleaded," Wright said. "It was very important for me—not just for me and my family and my two little girls—but also I wanted one more chance to be thankful of the support and the fans throughout the years.

"I wanted to salute them and thank them for having my back from 21 years old to 36 years old. It was important for me to meaningfully put the uniform on one more time. As much as I couldn't do it physically to just go out there and stand at third base even for a few innings, a couple of at-bats, just be able to thank the fans, to be able to blow some kisses to my girls on my way off the field. That was important to me, not just like a sendoff, but I genuinely wanted to thank the fans and show them how much I appreciated them over the years."

Wright, who became a special assistant in the Mets' front office, will likely see his No. 5 retired at Citi Field, eventually. His chances of enshrinement in the Hall of Fame are less certain, given the physical problems that curtailed his career.

It's a career that included seven All-Star selections, 242 homers, and a .296 batting average. Wright finished with a career WAR of 49.2. According to baseballreference.com, the average WAR for a Hall of Fame third baseman is 68.4.

"I can honestly look back and say I got the most out of my ability, a 6'0", 200-pound kid from Chesapeake, Virginia, that all he wanted to do was go to college and play baseball," Wright said. "When I look at it like that, I am very fulfilled. When I look at it what could have been, when I look at it that way, I am like, 'If I could have just stayed healthy, what could have been?' but it's pointless dwelling on it too much because when I look back on it I think I did everything I could to get out there on the field and play."

ACKNOWLEDGMENTS

The fun in writing this book was catching up with former Mets players, coaches, and executives, recording their memories and insights of events and seasons.

I'll start my thanks with Keith Hernandez, who not only spoke to me for this book, but was terrific enough to contribute a foreword, bringing his straight-shooting analysis onto these pages. Hank Azaria's contribution to the foreword, from the perspective of a long-suffering Mets fan, was also appreciated. Following Hank on Twitter, I knew his words would resonate with so many Mets fans who have been through the emotional wringer for so many years.

The chapter I had the most fun writing was on Johan Santana's no-hitter, and I'm thankful especially for the insights Bob Ojeda and my *New York Post* colleague Mike Vaccaro provided. There isn't a better sports columnist than "Vac," whose passion for the game is evident in his writing.

David Wright was nice enough to give me three separate interviews for this book. His perspective was certainly needed for any project that focused on this Mets era.

Another key contribution was Mike Piazza's. The Hall of Fame catcher sat with me for nearly an hour in Port St. Lucie, Florida, only days before spring training was shut down by COVID-19 in 2020, and offered a candid assessment of his Mets tenure and battles with Roger Clemens.

Tom Glavine, Billy Wagner, Edgardo Alfonzo, Al Leiter, Cliff Floyd, R.A. Dickey, LaTroy Hawkins, Jeff Francoeur, Michael Cuddyer, and Mike Baxter were among the former Mets players nice enough to return phone calls. Jacob deGrom, Zack Wheeler, and Noah Syndergaard showed interest in the project and weren't afraid to share their thoughts. Justin Turner always gave me a hardy welcome when the Dodgers were in town or I visited Dodger Stadium, and was more than happy to speak with me for the book.

Former Mets managers and executives who shared their memories and insights included Bobby Valentine, Terry Collins, Steve Phillips, Jim Duquette, Omar Minaya, J.P. Ricciardi, Adam Fisher, and Wayne Krivsky. Sandy Alderson, who returned to the Mets as team president in 2020, also offered perspective.

Two highly regarded pitching coaches, Rick Peterson and Dave Eiland, brought great insight. Former Mets hitting coach Kevin Long's recollections were also appreciated.

Gary Cohen's recall of events from 20-plus years ago is almost as uncanny as his talent in the Mets television booth. Cohen, Hernandez, and Ron Darling were invaluable resources to me.

I can't forget Jay Horwitz, the former Mets public relations guru and legend, who wasn't afraid to offer suggestions or help if I had trouble lining up a particular interview. Harold Kaufman and Ethan Wilson with the Mets were also assets.

The pages of the *New York Post* contain the best baseball coverage on the planet, and I am thankful to play for that team. Joel Sherman, Ken Davidoff, Dan Martin, and Vaccaro are All-Star teammates, with previous colleagues George King and Kevin Kernan not forgotten for their counsel. Sports editor Chris Shaw and his top lieutenants, Mark Hale and Dave Blezow, are equally appreciated.

A shout-out goes to Larry Schwartz for his mentorship and friendship over the years. Newsday baseball columnist Dave Lennon was a voice of positivity during the project.

Thanks to the folks at Triumph Books, led by Bill Ames and Michelle Bruton, for making this happen.

At home, thanks to Suzanne, Anthony, Bridget, and Cassidy for their patience as I spent more than a year immersed in this project, along with my daily duties covering the Mets. And, as always, thanks, Mom and Dad.